Praise for *Angel W*

"Corin Grillo's relationship with [...] When Corin's work came into m[...] [...]g already working with them, but her work testifies that there are levels to the angelic realm, and my life is now exploding with their graces on higher levels. My mind is blown daily!"

— **TruthSeekah**, author, podcaster, and hip-hop artist

"Corin Grillo's *Angel Wealth Magic* offers a link to awaken to your soul's birthright — spiritual affluence. Using the step-by-step practices outlined and the power of intention, you will have the angelic realm as your ally to create financial freedom. Corin generously shares her approach to connecting with the angelic realm."

— **Margaret Ann Lembo**, author of
The Essential Guide to Everyday Angels

"Corin Grillo lays out a road map to abolish self-doubt and maintain focus and clarity along the road to wealth. *Angel Wealth Magic* is everything you never knew you needed as a spiritual entrepreneur. It is a must-read for all who wish to walk the path of personal and professional expansion. You'll want to keep it close at hand!"

— **Leeza Robertson**, author of *Mermaid Tarot*

"*Angel Wealth Magic* offers the mind-expanding solutions we all need to create real, lasting wealth. It is a powerful resource for building and maintaining inner and outer wealth with ease, power, and purpose."

— **Kate Eckman**, award-winning author of
The Full Spirit Workout

"Heavenly help is an unconditional gift offered by a benevolent universe. Corin Grillo's lighthearted approach will jump-start your wealth endeavors as you tap into the celestial resources abundantly provided. I love how Corin brings in both the sacred and the practical. She will help you awaken the magic of your true nature and your oneness with Spirit."

— **Jean Slatter**, author of *Hiring the Heavens* and founder of the Higher Guidance Life Coach certification program

"*Angel Wealth Magic* is a delightful guide full of important information for those of us who want to enjoy the companionship of our best material security. Corin Grillo has written a wonderful book so that we can 'receive the biggest and best harvest possible' with 'all the goodness that the Divine has to offer.' Readers — enjoy every sumptuous word!"

— **Debbi Dachinger**, internationally bestselling author, award winning podcast host of *Dare to Dream with Debbi Dachinger*, and media interview coach

"Corin Grillo gives us a step-by-step guidebook to manifesting wealth at the highest level. She shows us that through working with the angels, we can heal and create space to allow our most magical adventure to unfold here on Earth. *Angel Wealth Magic* provides a fresh perspective on the influence angels have on our daily lives. It will shift your perspective about wealth and align you with the most magical force available to us all — Spirit."

— **Bill Philipps**, author of *Expect the Unexpected* and *Soul Searching*

ANGEL WEALTH MAGIC

Also by Corin Grillo

The Angel Experiment:
A 21-Day Magical Adventure to Heal Your Life

ANGEL WEALTH MAGIC

Simple Steps to Hire
the Divine & Unlock Your
Miraculous Financial Flow

CORIN GRILLO, LMFT

New World Library
Novato, California

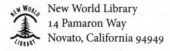

New World Library
14 Pamaron Way
Novato, California 94949

Text design by Tona Pearce Myers

Library of Congress Cataloging-in-Publication Data

Names: Grillo, Corin, date, author.
Title: Angel wealth magic : simple steps to hire the divine & unlock your
    miraculous financial flow / Corin Grillo, LMFT.
Description: Novato, California : New World Library, [2022] | Summary:
    "Teaches readers how to call upon benevolent spiritual forces to help
    them realize their personal, financial, and best-life dreams"-- Provided
    by publisher.
Identifiers: LCCN 2022036326 (print) | LCCN 2022036327 (ebook) |
    ISBN 9781608688128 (paperback) | ISBN 9781608688135 (epub)
Subjects: LCSH: Magic. | Angels. | Wealth.
Classification: LCC BF1621 .G747 2022 (print) | LCC BF1621 (ebook) |
    DDC 133.4/3--dc23/eng/20220825
LC record available at https://lccn.loc.gov/2022036326
LC ebook record available at https://lccn.loc.gov/2022036327

First printing, November 2022
ISBN 978-1-60868-812-8
Ebook ISBN 978-1-60868-813-5
Printed in Canada on 100% postconsumer-waste recycled paper

New World Library is proud to be a Gold Certified Environmentally Responsible Publisher. Publisher certification awarded by Green Press Initiative.

10   9   8   7   6   5   4   3   2   1

This book is dedicated to *mi familia*, all of them: my blood *familia*, my soul *familia*, and my invisible *familia* — my angels, my ancestors, and my allies in nature. Thank you for giving me the strength to stay alive long enough to serve others. You've loved me even when I didn't know how to love myself, and I'm forever grateful.

———————— ✤ ————————

Contents

INTRODUCTION: Magic Is Your Birthright 1

PART I: Wealth Foundations

CHAPTER 1: Defying the Odds 13

CHAPTER 2: Wealth Magic Pre-Party:
Setup to Supercharge Your Wealth Rituals 23
Practice: Your Magical Wealth Grimoire 30
Practice: Setting Your Intention 34
Practice: Your Wealth Altar 36
Practice: Working with Sigils (Magic Mirror) 42

CHAPTER 3: Archangels, Angels, and Allies
of the Wealth Realm Reference Guide 47
Practice: Quantum Invocation for Channel-Writing 64

CHAPTER 4: Transforming Your Wealth Demons 69
Practice: The Shame Purge Ritual 73
Practice: Owning Your Badassery 77
Practice: Kicking the Impostor Demon to the Curb 80
Practice: Self-Sabotage No Más! 83
Practice: Casting Away Confusion 86
Practice: Perfecting Imperfection 89
Practice: Quantum Invocation for Banishing Your Demons 90

CHAPTER 5: Magical Mindset Tricks of the Wealthy 93
Practice: Chatting with the Spirit of Money 96
Practice: Rocking Your Audacity 101
Practice: Optimism Uptick 104

Practice: Dreamin' Like a Honey Badger 107

Practice: Building Better Boundaries 110

PART II: Your 11-Day Wealth Ritual

Kick Start: Angelic Banishing Ritual 115

Guidelines for Your 11-Day Wealth Ritual 125

DAY 1 — Archangel Raziel: Open the Portal 127

DAY 2 — Nitika: Bring On the Cash 131

DAY 3 — Archangel Jophiel: Massive Optimism 135

DAY 4 — Rahnahdiel: Release Guilt, Shame,
and Unworthiness 139

DAY 5 — Sitael and Poiel: Reverse Misfortune,
Cancel Curses, and Become a Money Magnet 143

DAY 6 — Veuliah: The Right Kind of Wealth 149

DAY 7 — Harachel: Intellectual Abundance and Access to
Knowledge 155

DAY 8 — Vehuiah and Mumiah: Willpower and Leadership 159

DAY 9 — Yeyayel and Lauviah: Fame and Celebrity 165

DAY 10 — Hodahdiah and Sekeshiah: Big Manifesting and Big
Money 169

DAY 11 — Omael, Jupiter, and Cahetel: Magnify and Multiply
Your Harvest 173

CONCLUSION: Wealth Magic After-Party: How to Keep
Expanding Your Wealth Magic in Every Area of Your Life 179

Acknowledgments 185

About the Author 187

Introduction

Magic Is Your Birthright

Welcome to the wonderful world of angel wealth magic! Whether you are working a nine-to-five job, are an entrepreneur, or are just taking the first steps to becoming more independently wealthy, in this book you'll discover how to tap the divine spiritual power inside you and hire angels and spirit allies to unlock your next level of wealth. If you're looking for creative and mind-blowing solutions to attract fast cash, grow your bank account and your business, and build sustainable wealth in magical ways, then you've been guided to the right book.

The kind of magic you'll learn here isn't the Vegas-sideshow kind of magic. It's traditional magic, rooted in the practices of seekers, mystics, and magicians for millennia. It's fun, it's simple, and — most importantly — it works.

Unfortunately, magic has gotten a lot of bad press over the last few years and has been too easily dismissed as "new age" or "woo-woo," but nothing could be further from the truth. Magic is a powerful, ancient, and practical solution to hack some of life's most stubborn problems. For thousands of years, humans have used their natural and powerful connection with the invisible world to not just *survive* but *thrive* under even the harshest conditions.

Early humans understood that the natural world around them wasn't something to be claimed, exploited, and conquered. They recognized the living, breathing essence woven into the trees, animals, sky, plants, water, and every being, uniting all of life. They knew that the world was alive. They understood that this force was to be honored, respected, and befriended. When humans were aligned with this relationship and learned how to harness this natural power, they could be guided to water, shelter, and food, as well as receive other kinds of blessings to help them thrive along the way.

Sadly, due to influences like colonization, the rise of materialism, and the suppression and demonization of indigenous and magical practices by organized religions, many of us have lost our natural connection with real magic. We have forgotten our mystical nature and have forgotten how to forge an authentic and supportive bond with Spirit. But all was not lost. The magic is still here, and it's hiding in plain sight. It's in your blood and bones. It's part of you.

No matter where you are from on the planet, your ancestors at some point were (or hopefully still are) deeply tied to their land and called on their allies in Spirit to come to their aid. They knew that the land and the divine benevolent beings around them were there to support them and help them flourish. As a matter of fact, one of the reasons you're alive today is because of this connection.

So, by learning how to create your own authentic relationship with benevolent forces like the angels and other invisible allies, and by learning how to harness this beautiful power, you too can thrive, just like your ancestors. Magic is in your DNA, and since you've found this book, I'm betting that it's your turn to remember. Magic is your birthright.

Not too long ago, the angels brought me back to the magic of my own spiritual nature. It's my hope that through the wealth-ritual process you'll find in this book, you will discover your magic too.

What Are Angels, and How Can They Help?

Angels are traditionally considered messengers of God. Their name derives from the Hebrew word *mal'akh*, which means "messenger." However, I want you to know that thinking of angels simply as "messengers" doesn't quite cover the profound ways in which angels can support you.

In traditional Western magic and other mystical systems, it's believed that angels can also help you awaken to your own soul and divine nature. Angels can help you become more authentically aware of the Divine, unveil your spiritual gifts, and discover your own divine purpose and mission. Working with angels can put you in contact with your true soul's voice and allow you to find deeper meaning in your life. This is what the angels have done for me — and for countless others I've coached over the years.

In this book, you'll meet some of my favorite angels and allies of wealth. Many of these angels and allies have been called upon by mystics and magicians for centuries to not simply attract cash but also create the proper mental and emotional states to inspire them to turn their biggest dreams into realities. I believe that your best and highest vision for wealth is often linked to a deep sense of mission and purpose. I want to invite you to open your mind to this concept now, so that you can hold the intention that the work you are about to perform through this ritual is more than just money attraction. It can also be an opportunity for you to lean into the deeper query of *who you are* and *why you came here* as a soul inhabiting that cool meat suit of yours.

Message from the Angels

The angels want this book to support and encourage heart-centered humans, leaders, teachers, healers, and entrepreneurs to step into their power and to be generous with sharing their service and their medicine with others in bigger and broader ways. They want you to know that the extraordinary times we are living in require extraordinary leaders. You may not currently identify as a leader, but that doesn't mean you aren't one. There are many folks on the planet who secretly have a sense that they are here to help, to share a message, to teach, to heal, or to provide some kind of amazing service to others and make the world a better place. Do you have this sense about yourself? If so, the angels want me to let you know, while we have your attention, that it's time for you to start listening to that small voice inside you, your intuitive voice — the voice that says you have more to offer than meets the eye. They want you to open to the vision of what your life could become when you fully show up, let yourself expand, and allow yourself to follow these dreams until they become a reality.

When I invoked the angels and asked them for the first words they'd like me to share with you, these are the whispers that stirred in my heart:

> *This book is an invitation. It's an invitation from us, your angels, to beautiful humans like you to accept all the gifts that life has to offer you. One of those gifts is that of inner and outer wealth. We, your angel team, ask that you open your heart, let go of the struggle, and say "Yes!" to receiving the bounty that surrounds you and is within you. You are deeply loved, you deserve to be happy, and we want to help you. Welcome us into your life and let us help.*

I've found over the years in working with angels that when they give you an invitation, it's always a good idea to say yes to it. Enlisting the angels to support your dreams can bring powerful magic into your life and, yes, even to your bank account.

When I first encountered the angels, I had no idea of the extent to which they would come to support me, my family, my purpose, and even my financial flow. Much to my amazement, some of the most extraordinary miracles that I've witnessed have been financial. As a matter of fact, with the help of some of the methods you'll learn in this book, I miraculously attracted an unexpected $150K within two weeks. And you best believe that I didn't just say yes to that — I said, "hell yes!" I want you to have an opportunity to say "hell yes!" to miraculous sums of cash flowing your way too.

Lose the Baggage

Before we go much further, I want to have a little chat with you. One of the things I've noticed about nice, spiritually minded folks is that often they are a little shy about and resistant to claiming more cash in their lives. The perception is that somehow having a motivation to be wealthy will make them seem "less spiritual." Is this you? Do you secretly feel that having extraordinary amounts of cash is somehow "unspiritual"? Do you feel a little guilty about wanting more? I sure hope not, but if you do, you're not alone. It's time to check that mindset at the door, because thinking like that will keep good spiritual folks like you cashless.

Additionally, if you're worried that wanting to be wealthy is somehow shallow or greedy or that Spirit is looking down on you for having such "earthly desires," you can rest assured that your divine team isn't judging you. Spirit has helped us with things like food, shelter, and other resources from the beginning of time. Cash is no different. It's the currency of our age, and if there's one thing I've learned about angels over the years, it's that what they want most for you is that you be taken care of so that you can feel peace and be happy. Happiness is contagious, and when you are feeling safe, secure, and happy, it inspires others to be happy too.

The angels want you to learn how to ask for their help and hire them for even the most mundane aspects of your life. They want to help you learn how to dream bigger and detox from the old paradigms of lack, negative thinking, and feelings of unworthiness. They also want you to know that having economic power is just as beautiful as having spiritual power. You and your dreams deserve to be funded so that you can support the causes you believe in, serve others, and have the essential resources to make the world a better place. Ain't no shame in that game.

What to Expect When Expecting Angels

Whether you are looking for $200 or $200 million, the steps you will learn here can help you magically attract extraordinary opportunities, cash, and resources, and more importantly, shift your mindset so that you feel more supported and empowered to turn your biggest dreams into a breathtaking reality. I have witnessed clients tripling their annual income, getting $80K of their debts magically forgiven, doubling their number of weekly clients, and even better, experiencing radical improvements in their sense of safety and well-being. All of this happened within three to six months of completing this angel wealth ritual.

The practices that I offer also give you a real opportunity to improve your relationship with money, shed your money worries, gain powerful insights into what's blocking you from success, and help you heal from financial trauma. I've seen all of the above happen with this kind of magical work, and it's always pretty incredible when it does.

I also want to mention that if you're new to this stuff, you may be a little skeptical about the reality of angels. That's totally OK. I didn't used to fully believe in them either. The good news is that you don't have to in order for them to help you. Why? Because the angels believe in *you*, that's why. You don't have to be religious or even a full-on angel believer for this kind of angel magic to work for you. However, my hope is that by the end of working this magical wealth-attraction process, there will be no doubt left in your mind that angels are not just *real* but also willing, ready, and able to help you succeed.

All that's required for this kind of wealth magic to start working for you are these four magical basics:

- **Open-mindedness.** Stay open to the possibility that magic and angels are real.
- **Desire.** Have a heartfelt desire to grow your wealth.
- **Curiosity.** Look at the world with childlike curiosity and imagine what's possible for you.

- **Commitment.** Commit to this magical wealth-attraction ritual process to the end.

These four things can be enough to get you some pretty awesome results. So, if you can wholeheartedly show up with curiosity and commitment, then the angels can show up for you and meet you there.

It's my deepest hope that you enjoy the wealth magic journey that the angels and I have created for you in these pages. Indulge in these practices, play with them, complete the eleven-day ritual in part II of the book, and keep yourself open to new financial insights, opportunities, and inspiration along the way. Your magical wealth wonderland awaits.

Part I

WEALTH FOUNDATIONS

Chapter 1

Defying the Odds

If you had told me years ago that I would be writing an angel book on wealth, I would have thought that either you were on drugs or I was on drugs. Based on who I was back then, it would probably have been the latter. But here I am doing what I would have deemed impossible, and of course, I have the angels to thank for that.

If you've read my previous book, *The Angel Experiment*, then you know that I first encountered the angels through a miracle that set me on my extraordinary journey toward manifesting a life beyond my wildest dreams. Since that first miracle, I have continued to witness miracle after miracle in my life and in the lives of the folks I serve all over the world.

One of the most spectacular ways in which the angels have helped me over the years has been the radical expansion and multiplication of my own wealth. Of course, I'm not the wealthiest person out there by any stretch. I won't be booking a seat on the next private space-shuttle excursion anytime soon, but for someone from my background, the connections, success, and wealth I've experienced since working with the angels are astonishing. Miraculous even.

To offer you an idea of how astonishing this is, let me give you the quick skinny on who I am and a bit about where I'm from.

I'm a half Chicana and half Puerto Rican woman who didn't come from money. As a matter of fact, I had so little cash for a time in my younger years that I lived in one of the *barrios* of Los Angeles in a former crack house in an alley within an alley within an alley. Yes, you had to drive through three alleys to get to my house. Did you even know that was possible?

I lived in the Sangra and Lomas gang territory, with frequent drive-by shootings, drug running, and the like. To add fuel to the fire, my mother passed away when I was a teenager, which sent me on a very serious path of self-destruction. Even though I was a college student by day, I struggled by night with all the worst drugs, along with alcohol and depression. I even had a tiny adventure in jail because of these struggles.

You get the picture, right? Have you seen the stats on the upward mobility of poor, depressed brown women with drug problems and a little jail time? Yup, they're pretty dang low. There was nothing in my early history to indicate that I could have the life, the career, and the wealth that I have today.

In fact, one of the inspirations for me to write this book was that I manifested an extraordinary $150K back in 2020, during the first big Covid lockdown, by drawing upon the magical methods I share with you here. I don't usually like to throw numbers around publicly, but I'm compelled to divulge this financial miracle to you so that you know what's possible by using this kind of wealth magic.

Back in 2020, I struggled with navigating my work–home life balance. My role as CEO of my own business was in direct conflict with suddenly having two kids schooling from home full-time during Covid. Like so many parents out there, I made the decision to reduce my work hours and focus on helping my family navigate this new, extra-bizarre era as gracefully as possible.

But then I somehow had to try to make up for the loss of income. So what did I do? I did what I always do when I need to solve a big, juicy mind-f*ck of a problem. I asked the angels for help, and they inspired me to do some wealth magic. I dug deep into my magical arsenal and created a wealth ritual to help me attract $200K. I thought that amount was a serious long shot but decided to ask anyway.

Within two weeks of completing that ritual, I received an email saying that I qualified for a $150K extra-low-interest business loan — as in virtually free money. I couldn't believe my eyes, mainly because I didn't remember ever applying for a $150K loan. Wouldn't you remember if you asked someone for $150K? I was so baffled that I asked my hubby if he somehow managed to apply for that amount. He didn't do it either.

Then I remembered my wealth ritual and realized, yet again, how over-the-top amazing and miraculous working with angels can be.

That night I went outside in my backyard to do a gratitude ceremony. I lit a fire, made some offerings, and thanked the Creator, the angels, my ancestors, and Spirit for always showing how wildly creative they can be when supporting me.

As I sat by the fire, I thought of the parents around the world trying to homeschool and work at the same time. I thought of all the folks who lost their jobs during lockdown. I thought of the small-business owners who were struggling to keep their businesses alive. And I thought of all the marginalized folks out there who even without Covid were never given the chance for a hand up. It became clear that the miracle that just "happened" to my family wasn't meant for me to keep to myself. I realized that I had an obligation to share this wealth magic with others so they could learn how to defy the odds with the incredible power of angel magic. That's why I wrote this book.

So, why am I telling you all this? To brag? Nope. I'm telling you this because I want you to know that angels are amazing helpers when it comes to hacking the system, breaking through barriers, healing from the past, and living abundantly in the world. They can help you become an honest-to-goodness life hacker.

I wholeheartedly believe that the angels can do for you what they did for me no matter what walk of life you're from. You don't have to have been born with a silver spoon in your mouth or feel like a special person. In fact, it doesn't matter if you officially feel like you suck. You can even be terrible at managing your cash, and it *still* doesn't matter. Angel wealth magic gives all of us equal access to miraculous resources no matter our skin color; how much money we have; our gender, gender identity, or sexual preference; what country we're from; or what caste, class, or tribe we were born into.

I want you to know that your wealth story isn't over. Your wealth story could be just beginning. The angels and your spiritual allies can and will help you defy the odds in your life, career, or business and will work overtime to get you to your next level of wealth. Again, an open heart, an open mind, and a willingness to commit to the process are all that's required for this kind of magic to start working for you.

How This Book Can Help You Defy the Odds

Each and every prompt, practice, and ritual in this book is designed to support you to expand your wealth and help you defy the odds. Here are some highlights of things that you will learn and encounter in the upcoming pages:

- How to powerfully invoke and harness the power of ancient wealth magic angels and allies
- How to dispel your "inner demons," or the unconscious blocks that may be keeping you from your full wealth-attraction potential

- A reference guide to all my favorite badass wealth angels and allies
- Journal prompts and exercises designed to help you align your heart, mind, and body with the energetic field of wealth
- An eleven-day ritual to help supercharge your wealth attraction

In addition, you can access my Angel Wealth Magic website (AngelWealthMagic.com/Resources) with hundreds of downloadable wealth affirmations, downloadable MP3s, and other supportive resources that will help you align with abundance and keep your mind focused on wealth awesomeness along the way.

From this point on, I want you to think about each page and each practice included in this book as part of your wealth ritual. Each practice builds upon the ones before it to enhance the power of the 11-Day Wealth Ritual that you will find in part II.

I also want you to understand that just by opening the book, you've already set some wealth goodness into motion. The angels and allies of wealth are already standing by and are ready to begin working with you. They are designed for this wealth-attraction stuff. And so are you.

Growing Your Wealth Garden

While training others in the process of angel wealth magic, I came to understand that moving beyond the simple manifestation of fast cash and into the generation of sustainable wealth requires deep inner exploration and a mindset upgrade. As a psychotherapist, I have a natural fascination with the mind and the unconscious. I like to ponder how our mental architecture and belief systems either support or limit our ability to manifest our deepest desires. Sometimes we don't even realize that these beliefs are there because we've had them our whole lives — usually inherited or adopted from our ancestors, families, communities, and cultures. Because we pick these things up so young, we tend to make assumptions about ourselves and our lives based on these beliefs (often lies) and consider them to be true.

Let's imagine it this way: Think of your maximum, ultimate, next level of wealth as if it's a beautiful, lush garden overflowing with bounty. The birds are singing. The bees are buzzing, and all the fruits and veggies are plentiful, succulent, juicy, and ripe. When your inner wealth garden is hopping like this, it means your cash quotient is overflowing with goodness and your bank accounts are flush with resources. You have officially reached your next level of wealth.

Now imagine that your inherited belief systems about money are the soil for this wealth garden. The quality of your beliefs will either create fertile ground for your wealth seeds and magical effort to grow or create a toxic environment where your magical wealth seeds struggle to take root. Toxic beliefs will strangle your every attempt to reach your next level of wealth.

If on a subconscious level, your inner wealth garden is full of weeds and the soil is toxic, no matter what you do, no matter how hard you work, you will feel like you're financially stuck. Those mental weeds will suck the vitality out of your wealth garden and block your ability to have a fertile and bountiful life. I call them the Wealth Blockers, or WBs.

Wealth Blockers are like invisible condoms that prevent your wealth seeds from spreading and taking root in even the most fertile soil. They are the subconscious negative beliefs you inherited from society and your ancestors that keep you from manifesting your next-level wealth, even when you work really hard at it.

Do you ever feel like you take two steps forward and three steps back when you are trying to get ahead in life? Yeah, those are the ol' WBs bouncing you back. They are really good at what they do, but please don't lose hope. Ever. The invisible barrier that they create isn't impenetrable. When you think about it, even real condoms are only about 98 percent effective, right? Some of us are living proof of that.

Luckily, because the Divine is so cool, you have been given a wonderful angelic team to help you pull the mental weeds in even the most toxic soil in your mind. They can help you pierce through the invisible mental condom, so that the seeds of your heart's deepest desires for wealth, love, and joy can penetrate the fertile soil of Creation, and your biggest, most beautiful dreams can finally be birthed into the world.

So the question is, how can you identify and pull the mental weeds that are essentially keeping your wealthy life on lockdown? Well, there are lots of ways, really, but my favorite happens to be right between your ears: mindset magic, of course.

Besides the 11-Day Wealth Ritual in this book, you will also find exercises and practices that will allow you — with the help of the angels — to identify some of your mindset blind spots and magically shift some of the key thoughts, beliefs, and patterns that may be stopping you from attaining your next level of wealth. You'll get a chance to "pull the weeds" out of your wealth garden so that the magical wealth seeds that you plant throughout this ritual can actually take root and flourish. All of this is preparation that culminates in the eleven-day ritual, where you can apply everything you have learned. Say goodbye to the WBs.

The energy and commitment that you put into your magic in the beginning is often reflected in your results at the end. Enjoy this process. Take your time. Do the practices. Be curious about the mysteries that you may discover along the way, and get ready to officially begin your wealth magic ritual.

Chapter 2

Wealth Magic Pre-Party

Setup to Supercharge Your Wealth Rituals

Let the magic begin! It's finally time to jump-start your badass wealth magic journey. Can you feel the wealth magic vibes flowin'? I know I do, and the angels and I are excited to walk with you every step of the way.

The journey you are about to embark upon will be unique to you; there truly isn't a one-size-fits-all approach to working this powerful magic. Each person creates their own path with the help of the angels.

How do I know? Well, I have a little story for ya. I've shared some of my experiences with angels in this book and in *The Angel Experiment*, but I haven't told you about how I came to love magic. I first began learning about magic in my early twenties. A few years after my mother died, I had a powerful mystical experience that unleashed the flow of my first wave of spiritual juices. This experience set me on a journey that eventually led me down the path of Western traditional magic.

At a spiritual bookstore, I stumbled upon a flyer for a modern mystery school of magic. I soon was initiated into the school and eventually lived there. In this school we dove deep into magic, of course, but also Kabbalah, astral projection, ritual, manifesting, meditation, tarot, and a variety of other spiritual and mystical subjects. These days, none of the things that I just mentioned seem particularly controversial, but back then, even yoga was considered pretty dang fringe.

While living at the school, which we called "The Abbey," we woke at 5:30 with the sunrise, did our morning rituals, went off to our day jobs, where we would put our magic to the real test, and then came back to the school and continued with our magical operations. It was like living as a monk, but magic-style. During this time, I completely dedicated my life, from sunup to well past sunset, to magical study; I really honed my magic to help me break through my limitations.

After four long years of dedication to the magical path, it was time to move on. I'd learned a ton about magic, and had some pretty cool results manifesting along the way, but something was still missing. I was still a mostly miserable person, and I still struggled a lot to find meaning in a life that felt hopelessly meaningless. Because of this, I became disillusioned with magic and let the entire practice go for a while.

It wasn't until the angels entered my life in my midthirties, and I witnessed an amazing, life-changing miracle, that I came back to magic. On that transformative day, out of nowhere, I watched a bird drop from the sky and crash-land on the ground directly in front of my car. Rather than struggle, the bird, which had a broken wing, miraculously divided itself into three healthy birds and flew away. I know, it sounds a little over-the-top, right? Yeah, that's why I wrote the full story in *The Angel Experiment*.

This miracle came during a very low point in my life, and it allowed me to see the beauty and truth in magical incidents. That's when the real healing began for me. And that's when I found the one missing magical ingredient that I had overlooked throughout my entire career as a magical lady monk: love — divine love and all the awesomeness that comes with it.

What I came to learn was that the best kind of magic always involves a big, juicy, open heart. It comes from an authentic desire to make a connection with something bigger than yourself. Call it the universe, God, Mother Nature, Gaia, Bob, Love, or whatever name suits you; when you create a real and palpable connection with the big It/They, and when you begin to see the Divine truly working for you — in nature, including the sky, birds, and trees; your relationships; and even your bank account — it changes the magic game altogether.

As you walk through this process of angelic wealth magic with me, I will draw on some practices from my time in the magic school and other deeply rooted forms of magic. I do this with a lot of love because I know that there's no greater magic out there than truly feeling the support of Spirit and of life itself, colluding to bring you the gifts and blessings of protection, love, joy, and, yes, even wealth.

So let's get you set up for success with wealth magic! In this chapter, I lay out some simple steps you can take that will help you grease your magical wheels a bit, prepare your space, jump-start your relationship with the angels, and set clear and powerful intentions for your wealth-attraction journey. The wealth magic process in this book will help you rewrite the money story you have lived by your whole life. If you have had a strained relationship with money in the past, this is an incredible opportunity for you to close out that tired old story and begin imagining what life looks and feels like when that money relationship is repaired and good to go.

Make the Choice

The life you are standing in right now has not come about by accident. A very mighty and mysterious power has shaped it, and I can guarantee that this mighty power is the primary reason why your love life, your bank account, your circle of friends, and even your career look the way they do. Because this book talks about a lot of spiritual concepts, you may be thinking that I'm about to blame the outcomes in your life on divine design, karma, fate, or some kind of high-level spiritual theory like this, but that's not what this is about. The mighty power that I'm alluding to is your power of choice. Your ability to make a choice is one of the most significant life-shaping tools that you have in your grasp.

Although the concept of making a choice is simple, it is one of the biggest keys to the success of your magic and, really, success in life. This life you are living didn't happen by chance; it happened by choice.

Before I go further, I want to be clear that what happened to you when you were a child *wasn't* your choice or your fault. Your life back then was an expression of the whims or choices of your caretakers. If you were surrounded by poverty or abuse growing up, that wasn't because of you, and you are not responsible for that. And specifically, because this is about wealth magic, you need to understand that you are also not responsible for any of your family's financial trauma or financial patterns that may have affected you as a child. You didn't choose any of that. Nor did you choose the unforeseen or disastrous events in your adult life that sent negative ripple effects into your bank account. What matters, however, is how you choose to respond to all that crap. You are responsible for the financial choices that you make now as an adult. Those choices do inform your financial outcome.

A couple of good questions to ask yourself here are:

- How is my upbringing still informing the choices, especially the financial choices, I make today as an adult?
- Do I make choices in life that still minimize my value, because I didn't feel valued in my family?
- What financial trauma have I had in the past that may be negatively impacting the financial choices I am making today?

Whatever your answers are, what's important now is how you choose to move on and heal from past traumas. And healing from the past can help positively guide your future financial life.

You may look around at your financial life and not immediately like what I'm saying here because that financial life may seem like a bit of a shit show. That's OK. We have all been in a shit show here and there, and I'm sure this isn't your first rodeo. I'm sure, for instance, that at some point you found your way out of debt when you really needed to. The question is, how did you do that? How did you get through the shit show? The simple answer is that you chose to do something differently. You chose to quit an old toxic job, get a new job, invest in a new education, pay down what you owed, move to a new city, develop a new income stream, or ask for help.

A magician understands that they have the option in every moment to *choose* differently — to choose a different trajectory. And essentially, that is what you are doing by deciding you want to learn how to work with angel magic to open up new portals to wealth. A magician strives to know and understand that the first power they employ in any magical act is making a clear and proactive choice to change their reality. They consciously choose to move away from victimhood and take radical responsibility for the conditions of their life. A magician is willing to take their power back from society, from their family of origin, or from the haters or the naysayers. They fully realize that they have the power to separate themselves from the struggles of the past and re-create their lives in accordance with their own beautiful vision, or their True Will.

The success of your wealth magic depends on the power of your choices, specifically the choice to be wealthy — *and mean it*. And mean it not just for a week or a month or a year, but for as long as it takes, even after you are done working the steps in this book.

Making the conscious choice to be wealthy can allow you to create an extraordinary shift inside yourself. You can open up to new pathways of being and thinking about yourself. You can learn to drop the old stories you've been telling yourself about your life and about money. So, if you are really ready to make a different choice in life — if you are ready to make the choice to be wealthy — then say this out loud: "I choose to be wealthy!"

Say it as if the angels are standing in the room right there with you (because they are). Say it over and over again until you feel like you really mean it. Get yourself revved up about it. Let your body feel the enthusiasm of it, and know that this choice is real and the first beautiful step of your wealth-making journey.

How does it feel to make the choice to be wealthy? What do you notice? Are you stoked? Is there a part of you still resisting? Take a moment to write down how it feels to make the choice to be wealthy. Don't have a place to write it down yet? Well, you will in just a minute. Keep reading.

PRACTICE

—— ⚕ ——

Your Magical Wealth Grimoire

Now that you have made the powerful and ultra-magical choice to be wealthy, you'll need a magical wealth grimoire — a magical journal of sorts. Your magical wealth grimoire can be either paper or digital, whichever works best for your lifestyle. It will be your go-to place to record all your magical findings, experiences, wealthy thoughts, inspirations, and successes along the way.

A grimoire is a key companion for most ancient and modern magicians. A magician understands that they can use their words as a powerful manifesting machine. They write in their grimoire often, using it not as a place to vent, like a traditional journal, but instead as a tool to magnify their magic and cocreate their new reality, wishes, and desires into being with the support of divine forces. I want you to think of yours as a vessel for magical creation. You can use the pages of this grimoire to write love letters to your Spirit team, to make pleas for divine intervention, and to recommit, over and over again, to your wealth-making journey. You can also use it to write down powerful thoughts, feelings, and affirmations; create wealth-inspired art; or write down your worries, concerns, and imagined limitations with respect to achieving your next level of wealth. As you discover limiting beliefs and new WBs, you can write them in your magical grimoire too and ask the angels to assist you in transforming them into feelings and thoughts of beauty, hope, and inspiration.

I should also mention that this kind of magic can ignite new ideas and inspiration from your Spirit team concerning how to attract more wealth in your life, so you will definitely want to pay attention and write all these revelations in your grimoire. You'll want to keep this grimoire with you most of the time, as you never know when a flash of divinely inspired genius is going to hit your sweet little noggin.

Throughout this book, I will give you grimoire prompts and exercises to boost your wealth magic and enhance the fertility of your wealth garden. However, there are a variety of ways you can use your magical wealth grimoire, so feel free to work with it however you see fit, as long as you work consistently with this awesome magical tool.

In case you need a little help getting started, here's a basic template for your magical grimoire. These questions and reflections will help you focus your magical mind daily on the task at hand — manifesting your next level of wealth. Before you begin, however, I want to be clear that this is not busywork. Think of these daily writings as a sacred and powerful aspect of your magical wealth creation.

Daily Prompts
for Your Magical Grimoire

- Say out loud: "I am truly wealthy." Contemplate this statement. Write down two ways in which your life already reflects a sense of wealth.

- What are you creating today? Write down how you desire to feel, how you want your day to go, and what outcomes you would like to experience.
- Name one success. Take a moment to write about and celebrate the success you are already having.
- What ideas, inspirations, signs, synchronicities, or magical happenings would you like to record?
- What is one sacred action step that you can take today to create more wealth?
- What are you grateful for? Authentic gratitude opens the portal to receiving more blessings.
- Do you need any help from your divine team today? If so, with what? Make sure to thank them for their support.
- Write down anything else that you want to record for the day.

Understanding Your *Why*

When you have big goals, dreams, and an awesome vision for your life, it goes without saying that more than likely it will take some serious time, energy, and investment. One of the secrets to turning your dreams into reality is finding a real, heart-centered motivation to make this goodness happen. You're reading this book, so it's already obvious that you're looking for a wealth uplevel, but have you taken the opportunity to truly understand why? Have you really thought about the benefits of having more cash in your life and the impact it would make?

When I ask folks why they are looking to attract more cash, most say that they want more money to pay off debt or pay their rent, mortgage, or other bills. And though, yes, these things are important, sometimes they are not quite sexy enough to get you fully motivated to make all the big stuff happen.

In this section, I want you to go a little deeper with the question of *why* you want more cash. The more you ask why, over and over again, the more you discover your underlying motivations for achieving that next level of wealth. Magic often works best when you are in touch with your deeper feelings surrounding your intention. I want you to feel lit up when thinking about having more cash in your life.

The best way to work through the *why* is to sit quietly, bust out your grimoire, and make a list. Ask yourself this question: "Why do I want to be wealthy?" Once you have your answer to that, then ask yourself: "Why else do I want to be wealthy?" Write that one down, and ask again, "Why else?" Do this six or seven times — ten times if you are feeling really frisky. I want you to let yourself feel the desire for wealth inside your body. Again, the point of this is to help you feel the emotion around your vision, from your heart.

Sometimes you will come across deeper desires to serve others or your family, or to be an inspiration for others. Maybe you want to buy your parents a house or build generational wealth for your children. Some of these *whys* may actually make you a little weepy. That's a good thing. You can really channel that emotion toward your magic. Make sure to review your *why* as often as you like to help you stay committed to your wealth vision.

PRACTICE

——————— ⚜ ———————

Setting Your Intention

Now that you are connected to the deeper reasons behind why you want to attract more wealth, you are ready to set an intention. Every solid magical ritual begins with a powerful intention. To be able to shift your wealth reality with angel magic, you will first need a strong vision of what you want to manifest. We already know that you are looking for more wealth, but have you considered how much? And when you need it? Before you write out your intention, answer the questions below to decide specifically how much money you are looking to attract and what you will spend it on.

1. Do you need some quick cash now? If so, how much, for what, and by when?
2. What is your monthly income goal? How much money would you like to see coming into your bank account or into your business every month? Write down the dollar amount in your grimoire.

3. How much income do you want to make in the next year? Write down that dollar amount in your grimoire.

4. How much wealth would you like to see coming in annually five years from now? Write down that dollar amount in your grimoire too.

These numbers will give you an initial road map for the next few years. Having a big target to aim for is always helpful, especially when you are looking to build sustainable wealth. Refer back to these numbers frequently and take the time to imagine them as a reality.

To create this intention, I want you to focus on either your quick cash goal (#1 above) or your monthly personal or business profit goal (#2 above) for the remainder of this book. You will also use this goal when you get to the eleven-day ritual in part II. We begin here because these are your immediate needs. However, after you have worked this full process once, you can go back to the ritual and work with the bigger numbers.

Now it's time for you to write out your intention. I've given you a simple intention-writing format below, but feel free to write yours however you see fit.

Dear Creator of All That Is, angels, and my other wealth allies,

It is my intention to manifest $_____ [insert amount of money] *by* _____ [state the day by which you would like to manifest this amount]. *I intend to use this money to* _____ [fill in the blank with how you will use it].

I also ask that you lift my fears, open the road toward sustainable wealth, and help me feel supported in magical and miraculous ways. I thank you for helping me, and I am ready to receive your blessings.

When you are finished writing this down, I want you to find a nice place either indoors or outdoors and call in the angels. Imagine they are with you, and read your intention out loud as if you are surrounded by these amazing helpers and there is standing room only.

If you are new to this angel magic stuff, it can feel a little weird in the beginning, but do it anyway. Stating your intentions out loud is a very magical act, and it can be fun too! When you call upon angels, you may actually sense or feel their presence with you, or you may not. Either way, it's helpful for you to read your intentions out loud to let the angels officially know that you are looking for some help.

If you want to take your magic up a notch and give your intention some extra power, you can make a copy of it and place it on a wealth altar.

PRACTICE

Your Wealth Altar

A wealth altar, or sacred space, can be used as an anchor point for your wealth magic to thrive. An altar is a small, dedicated area inside your home that is used almost like a doorway or portal to help open up communication with the Divine. Like most things in this book, have fun with this!

Altars can serve a variety of different purposes. Some people create altars to help them connect with ancestors. Others do so to help them attract love, bring protection, or manifest a new job. I include this step of creating a wealth altar because my experience has been that people deeply love having these sacred spaces in their home and they report receiving great healing, peace, and blessings from them.

Altars come in an array of shapes and sizes, and they don't have to be big or ornate. Yours can be a small spot on your nightstand or a giant bookcase full of amazing sacred objects. It really doesn't matter, as long as you dig it and are inspired by it. Your altar can be as simple as setting aside a space for a single candle or a check made out to "self" with the amount of cashola that you are attracting.

If you aren't in the mood to create a space inside your home, feel free to create one outside. Outside mini-altars can be just as beautiful, fun, and powerful. Also, if you want to go ultra-minimalist-style, or if you have cats or children in the house who might pull or knock objects off your altar, you can even create a portable wealth altar. To do this, simply place your inspired objects on a cloth, fold the cloth around the objects, tie it with a string or ribbon, and store it in a drawer until you want to bust it out again to work your magic. You can even fold up a page with your intention printed on it and place it in the cloth to help your magic grow.

Before you create a special wealth altar, I want you to first consider what images or symbols come to mind when you think about wealth. Are there any spiritual beings you associate with wealth? Whatever comes to mind, you can find a way to represent those images on your altar. You can print photos or put up cute statues. You can even include actual money or, as I mentioned before, write yourself a check for the amount you are looking to attract. Feel free to get creative. And most important, have mega fun creating your wealth altar! Here are some other objects that folks like to use to help them create an inspired wealth altar space:

- Candles
- Altar cloth
- Silk scarves
- Artwork
- Incense
- Flowers
- Feathers
- Crystals or gemstones
- Pictures, statues, or figurines of your fave angels, gods, goddesses, and animal or spirit guides
- Cashola (as long as you have trustworthy roommates, of course)

Create a wealth altar that feels meaningful to you, fill it with love, and remember to place your written wealth intention on it.

Here's a simple, fun way to work with your wealth altar on a daily basis:

1. Light a candle.
2. Call in your angels and allies of wealth.
3. Imagine them by your side and sense their presence.
4. Remind them of your intentions. Ask them for help, inspiration, clarity, support, strength, or whatever else you might need along the way. Ask them to remove anything that blocks you from your desired goal.
5. Thank them for listening.
6. Notice whether you feel different.
7. Write down anything you feel called to record from this experience (new ideas, intentions, and so forth) in your magical grimoire.

Working with your wealth altar like this is a very sweet and beautiful process. Do whatever feels right for you, and know that when you bring the sacred into even the smallest corner of your home, your *home* becomes sacred.

Now, I know that a lot of folks are busy. You may feel overwhelmed even thinking about making a wealth altar. Please, do this step only if it feels in alignment for you, but for Pete's sake, keep going. If a wealth altar doesn't feel like your jam right now, don't worry about it. People tend to love working with them, but some folks really don't want to bother. And that's OK.

Sacred Reciprocity

In case you are totally new to angels or the thought of having spiritual allies, I should mention that the best magic happens when you make the effort to build a relationship with them, just like with any new friend you want to spend more time with. I call this sacred reciprocity. Reciprocity, when it comes to angels and any other divinity, is all about not just taking from Spirit and asking for things but also giving back to Spirit through offerings. Indigenous people all over the world tend to remember this step, and more than likely, so did your ancestors. This keeps the relationship with Spirit and nature in balance; plus, it feels amazing to give back to these loving beings and to show gratitude when you ask for or receive support from both Spirit and nature.

I have found that making offerings to the angels or other divinities I work with opens up a deeper connection for love to flow. And as with building any new relationship, it's a wonderful way to put your best foot forward right from the start.

There are a variety of beautiful ways to make offerings. If you find that you really want to get to know a particular angel better, or you want to give them a big thanks for all their help, you can dedicate a special time and place to do the offering.

Here are some ideas for offerings to help you along, but know that your options are infinite. Always feel into your heart for unique ways to make your offerings. Let your intuition guide you to what feels natural to you.

As I mentioned earlier, your ancestors knew how to do this, which means that this knowing is already present in your blood and bones, whether you are conscious of it or not.

- **Burn incense.** Call in the angel and burn incense for them. Give them deep gratitude for their assistance and let them know that you are looking forward to getting to know them better.
- **Light a candle or build a fire.** Look into the candle flame or the fire as if it is an open door to the angel or spirit you want to connect with. Have a heartfelt, loving conversation with them and keep the candle safely lit for the day or allow the fire you built to burn out attended.
- **Sing.** This offering is not just fun but also really raises your vibes. There's a reason why cultures all over the world sing praises to the Divine with song. It's because it works. Choose an angel and sing them a song. It can be one you know or make up on the fly. If you think you are a crappy singer, sing anyway. The angels *love* it and couldn't care less if you don't sound like Whitney or Mariah — it's all about your heart. As long as your gratitude is heartfelt, then you are good to go.
- **Dance.** This is also a fun one, and opens your connection to your roots and ancestry.

You can even burn some calories while you are at it. Bonus! Dancing helps drum up the medicine and power from the earth into your body. It creates celebration energy, and Spirit loves to celebrate. And again, if you think you have no rhythm, it doesn't matter. Do it anyway if you feel it in your heart.

- **Draw.** You can call your angel in and create an art piece for them. This one is also great because you can use that art piece in the future as a portal to assist you in communicating with that particular angel.
- **Offer things that smell or taste good,** like flowers, cookies, or anything that you think is fragrant or delicious.

Again, use your intuition, and go from there. Oh, and one last thing: I highly recommend the great outdoors when rocking your offerings — it can be extra fun and extra powerful.

Have fun with your offerings and let the love flow!

PRACTICE

❖

Working with Sigils (Magic Mirror)

The sigil, or magic mirror, is another tool I would love for you to use along the way. Sigils help magicians hyperfocus their energy and magical intentions. Sigils are rooted in traditional magic, which I have modified here to create what I call a magic mirror practice to help you anchor into and embody your intention. This should open a more powerful communication channel with your angels. Think of the sigil like a calling card, a way to reach your angel.

There are a variety of ways to work with sigils. Every sigil usually begins with a circle, or concentric circles, and then some kind of design is drawn in the middle of it. Some have complex designs. Some are simple.

Over the years, I've heard a lot of different explanations for what the outside circle (or circles) represents. My favorite way of viewing it is to think of it as a portal, a window, a container for magic, and a womb from which magic can be birthed. For me, it represents all of the above.

Inside the circle(s), some magicians draw complicated symbols or ancient designs that represent specific deities, including angels. Some people just put words, names, or letters, written plainly or elaborately. Sometimes magicians simply intuit symbols for their magical operation and draw those images within the circle.

For this wealth magic ritual, we are going to keep things simple. Once we get to the eleven-day ritual, you will use the magic mirror in practices with a few of the angels. For now, to get a head start in learning how to work with a sigil and give your intention a magical boost, you can do the basic practice outlined below.

First, you'll need a blank sigil. Go to the resources page of this book's website to download and print a sigil template (AngelWealthMagic.com/Resources), or you can hand-draw your sigil circles based on the image below.

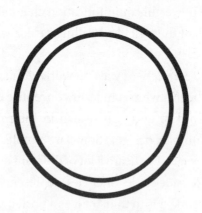

Steps for Working with Your Magic Mirror

1. In the center of the circle, write the dollar amount you are working to attract.

2. Stare at only the white space surrounding the dollar amount you wrote in the center, as if the sigil itself is a doorway or portal to the divine world or the angelic realm. While staring at the white space, remember your intention. Put emotion into it. Feel how much you want this and why you want this. Imagine that you are projecting this intention through the white space into the angelic realm.

3. Now stare at only the outer circle, and while

doing so, make the choice to attract money through magic — for example, affirm: "I choose to attract $5K through angel magic." You can say this out loud or in your head, whichever feels more powerful for you.

4. Look at the center of the circle again, but this time focus on the written dollar amount, not the white space. While you are staring at the number, imagine that the outcome has already come to pass — feel that your magic has worked and your cash has manifested in the present moment.

5. Look at the image in its entirety. As you focus your gaze, imagine yourself ten or fifteen years from now. Look back at this moment as if you manifested this amount years ago and have grown way past this intention. Imagine that you have all the cash you need. Fondly remember yourself today, doing this magic mirror practice for the first time, and celebrate how far you have come since then.

You can also make copies of your designs and put them in your sacred space or tape them on a bathroom mirror or wherever your gaze rests a lot so that you have a constant reminder of your wealth magic ritual and intention.

————————— ✤ —————————

Now that you have some of the basic steps that can help your magical wealth garden grow, it's time to meet the amazing team of angels and other allies to support you along your wealth-making journey. I want to introduce them to you before we start our eleven-day ritual. Ready to meet them? OK, let's fly.

Chapter 3

Archangels, Angels, and Allies of the Wealth Realm Reference Guide

A re you ready to officially meet the angels and allies that will be supporting your magical wealth-attraction journey? I know they are ready to meet you!

What these angels and other divinities all have in common is that they've been hired for generations to help humans like you magically manifest wealth and inner characteristics that support a wealthy lifestyle. Though there are more angels of wealth than just the ones I introduce in this chapter, this list will give you a strong start for your angel wealth magic adventure. Some of these are archangels, while others are ancient angels, allies, and divinities found in the Bible or other, older sacred or magical texts.

I also want to note that the descriptions I present here aren't meant to be the ultimate truth on these angels, but they will give you a nice framework to help you start your personal magical work with them. Each angel possesses far more abilities and powers than what I have listed here. As I mentioned earlier in the book, I always recommend that you develop your own personal relationship with the angels in order to discover more about their qualities and how they can support your vision for your life. Developing a personal relationship with angels isn't just fun; it's also helpful in developing your own power and spiritual strength.

So the question is, how do you build a relationship with angels? Well, I have some ideas for you. First, as you read through this list of angels, open up your "Spidey senses" and notice which angels intuitively seem to jump out at you or resonate with you. Often, the angels you are intuitively guided to are those that can help you with your unique recipe for wealth making. At the end of this chapter, you'll learn a potent practice for calling on these angels, and many of them show up again in the next two chapters, as well as the eleven-day ritual.

Now that you have your spiritual eyes peeled, have a pen and paper handy, and let's dive into the angelic who's who of magical wealth manifesting.

Wealth Magic Angels and Allies

Aladiah (eh-LAH-dee-ah)*

Aladiah can help you with both spiritual and material abundance. Score! This angel can also help shield you

---

* True confession: While these pronunciation guides represent how I say the angels' names, the names themselves are from ancient Hebrew, and I can't claim that these pronunciations are perfectly accurate in all cases. However, I *can* confirm that the angels respond when I pronounce their names this way!

from the negativity of others or negative responses to the work you do. Just say no to haters with this angel in your corner. Aladiah also has amazing healing power and can assist with regeneration in both physical and financial health arenas. If you are starting a new project, this is a great angel to work with.

Cahetel (CAH-het-el)

This angel can help you drive away darkness or "evil" in all its forms. This includes offering protection from negative influences, both human and spiritual. They* also support easy progress and success, and can help you adapt and change your lifestyle to one more conducive to wealth. Cahetel can, in general, help you attract cash and long-term wealth.

Daniel (DAN-ee-el)

The angel Daniel can help you gain clarity if you get confused and have a hard time making small or big decisions. This angel can give you confidence in your choices and

---

* Angels encompass both male and female qualities, and they may appear genderless or as different genders at different times. To reflect this, I generally use *they/them* to refer to the angels. When it comes to the archangels, many have traditional gender representations, some going back to the Bible and other ancient texts, which I've honored in this book. However, you may experience them as a different gender or gender fluid. Gender is kind of a human thing! It's becoming less relevant in the collective, and a lot of shifts are happening. People are reporting even Archangel Michael coming to them as a she. What is true of all the angels is that they embody and vibrate the unconditional love of Source, regardless of gender.

reduce the anxiety or heavier emotions that might come along with any decisions you are struggling to make.

Elemiah (ell-em-EE-ah)

This angel can help you eliminate negativity and bad thoughts. If you are feeling anxious or worried about a perceived problem and you can't relax, this angel can bring you a sense of calm and optimism. Elemiah can also help you recover from past problems or perceived failures and feel hopeful about life and your future again. In addition, they can support you as you commit to your own work and your mission and help give you the energy to take action toward your goals and dreams.

Hachashiah (hah-CHAH-she-ah)

If you have a beautiful idea or project that might feel too big for you, work with this angel to help get clarity and move forward with grace, even if your goal seems a little too ambitious. Hachashiah can lend a hand when you are feeling overwhelmed, helping you push through the confusion so you can take decisive action.

Hahahel (hah-hah-HELL)

Sometimes we stop ourselves from playing big because we are afraid of negativity from other people. This angel is great at helping you deal with bullies in your immediate circle or with haters and trolls. If there is an overtly cruel person in your life who has a problem with boundaries and is harshing your vibe, Hahahel has the power to stop this enemy in their tracks. Call on them if you need protection or a shield in the moment, and ask that the bullying or attacking not recur in the future.

Hahaiah (hah-HAH-ee-ah)

Hahaiah provides the power to overcome adversity. If you had a rough upbringing or are currently experiencing a tough time, this angel can give you the strength to endure the hardship or help put a stop to it. The kinds of challenges that this angel can lend a hand with are varied, so if you feel like you are hitting a wall or are dealing with stubborn folks who are bringing you down, work with this angel to help you move past this hurdle and get to the other side.

Hakamiah (hah-KAH-me-ah)

If you are actively being oppressed or come from a marginalized group, this angel can help you get your power back from the person, people, or situation that is oppressing you. This angel can also bring you opportunities to manifest wealth and showcase your authentic gifts so you appear in a noble light and your work is more esteemed. Hakamiah can be of assistance in attracting loyal folks into your circle who believe in you and your dreams, and can bring you helpful people who want to lift you up instead of tear you down. They can also help *you* stay loyal to who you are and believe in your dreams so that you have the willpower to turn those dreams into reality.

Harachel (HAH-rah-chel)

This angel can help you be magnetic and make an impact with your gifts and talents. If you desire to be more influential within your circle or with your clients or audience, this angel can help you stand out in the crowd. Harachel can also help increase your smarts and your intellectual understanding of any situation. They can aid you in being more productive with your work and turn your brilliant, big ideas into wealth-making opportunities.

Hariel (HAH-ree-ell)

If you feel too paralyzed to take action on your dreams, this angel can unblock your flow and help you gain traction. They can enhance your ability to successfully follow through with your magical vision. In addition, Hariel can help you improve your chances of success and magnify your magical results.

Hayiel (HAH-yee-ell)

This angel can help you receive amazing, world-changing ideas and muster the audacity and strength to execute your plans and turn them into reality. They can assist with strengthening your resolve to pursue your dreams and bring your gifts, message, and service to the world. Hayiel can also give you the divine inspiration to embrace your role as a leader of your movement.

Hodahdiah (haw-DAH-dee-ah)

This angel helps you become a manifesting machine. They can assist you in focusing your energy on what you are seeking, so that you are more likely to receive results. Hodahdiah can help you bring your desired outcomes from the dreaming stage more swiftly into material reality.

Lauviah (LAU-vee-ah)

Lauviah can help you find loyal fans for your work and expand your reach so that more folks will be exposed to your talents and gifts. This angel can boost your enthusiasm about sharing your work with a broader audience and help you push through shyness to make yourself more visible. They can give you the confidence you need to shine like the star you are.

Lelahel (leh-lah-HELL)

This angel can help bring you good fortune in all your projects and pursuits and enhance your overall happiness. Lelahel supports strong ambition and creative endeavors and can help you reignite your motivation when the energy wanes or you lose momentum.

Mumiah (moo-ME-ah)

This angel can offer you protection during any magical ritual. They can shield your project from negative energy or influences that may want to steer you away from your commitment. Mumiah can help you cultivate the power, determination, motivation, courage, and audacity to take action on your delightful ideas for wealth and other projects and turn them into reality.

Nememiah (nem-em-EE-ah)

If you desire to quell your money worries and develop a more loving relationship with money, angel Nememiah can help you feel a whole lot better. They can help you let go of your fears and open to more financial flow. They can also inspire you to open up to your strategic genius and become truly devoted to your mission.

Nitika (nee-TEE-kah)

This spirit in traditional Western magic is not an angel but a celestial being said to be an embodiment of the Virtues, a group of celestial beings that support miracles and manifestation. Gentle and loving yet extremely powerful, Nitika can masterfully help you unlock quick cash, rediscover forgotten funds, and attract resources. They can also help applications for loans run smoothly and can open the door for unexpected cash, bonuses, and windfalls to come your way. Magical money manifestation from Nitika can happen quickly, within one to two weeks, and often they overdeliver on financial requests.

Omael (AW-muh-ell)

This angel can help you heal from any financial trauma you may have experienced in the past or are experiencing currently. Omael can help you feel productive and successful, regardless of your history. They can also boost your willpower to persevere through adversity when you feel exhausted and can help you find the energy to pursue your projects, dreams, and mission or establish or grow your business.

Pedahiel (ped-ah-HEE-ell)

This angel can help you feel appreciated and get acknowledgment from others. If you want to increase the level of respect you receive from friends, family, colleagues, followers, clients, or even loan officers, then summon this angel. Pedahiel gives you a sense of beautiful inner strength and will help others sense this power and quit bothering you. This angel also has the power to repel enemies and attract fans and admirers — so juicy! What's more, they can help you appreciate all that you already have and feel "good enough." This angel bolsters your courage to take a leap of faith. Pedahiel helps you be seen as a winner and feel rewarded for your efforts.

Poiel (PAW-ee-ell)

Poiel can help you open the road to fortune and good financial luck. They can also help you manifest your heart's deepest desires, feel hopeful about your financial future, and convert your talents and unique creative gifts into fame, fortune, and celebrity. This angel can help you become admired, revered, and respected in your chosen field — especially those career paths and projects that sing to your soul.

Raduriel (rad-OR-ee-ell)

This is an angel of creativity that can stop you from self-sabotage. They can help you raise your vibe when you have sunk into emotionally dark places, reigniting your passion and inspiring you to create a life in alignment with your heart's deepest desires. Raduriel can reconnect you with enthusiasm for your life and your projects and help you sing your "song" creatively in the world.

Rahnahdiel (rah-NAH-dee-ell)

Rahnahdiel is not just one angel but is said to embody the powers of several angels. Rahnahdiel can help you dissolve the shame, guilt, or unworthiness that may secretly be undermining your ability to get more out of life. They are a redeemer who can support you in bypassing old programming of "sinfulness." They can also help you embrace and accept yourself as you are.

Sekeshiah (sek-esh-EE-ah)

Think of abundance in all its forms when it comes to this angel. Sekeshiah combines the powers of many angels in order to "fertilize" your inner wealth garden with the energy of massive abundance. This being also gives you a sense that all your needs are being met effortlessly. They can stamp out any fears you hold related to money and allow you to open up to the infinite flow of abundance all around you. This angel can help you feel like you are blessed and that everything you put your energy into can and will turn into gold with ease.

Sitael (SIT-ah-ell)

This angel can help you reverse a run of bad luck, along with curses and negative energy. If you have experienced a series of misfortunes, this angel can assist you in transforming this pattern and expanding what's possible for you in life. Additionally, they can help you have integrity with your words and keep promises to yourself and others. Sitael can also support you in expanding the scope of the work you do and can open the door to the next-level, upgraded version of your life.

Vehuiah (veh-HOO-ee-ah)

Vehuiah can help you understand yourself as a leader on a deeper level and guide you in becoming an innovator in your field. They can help you move past the fear of rejection and give you an overall boost of courage to put yourself out there, unabashedly offer your services, and ask others for help. They can also give you the energy to persevere through the doldrums and complete a task. This includes tasks where you feel "too small" or where you might feel like an impostor.

Veuliah (vee-OO-lee-ah)

Often seen as an angel of joy and abundance, Veuliah can help you attract wealth that comes from the heart and inspire you to do work that feels good, serves others, but can also reward you financially. This angel can help you block out negative people and the haters along the way so you can stay strong, noble, and committed to your course of awesomeness.

Yeyayel (yeh-YAH-ee-ell)

This angel can help you attract fortune and wealth and enhance your reputation within your community and beyond. Think success, fame, and celebrity. They can assist you in developing that inner sense of leadership and moving past shyness or introversion so that you can share your creativity and service with your community and the wider world. They can also help you become a master negotiator, so if you have to sign or create a contract for business or anything else, work with Yeyayel. They can help these negotiations run more smoothly.

Archangels
Chamuel (CHAM-you-ell)

This archangel is widely known as the angel of peace. They can help you let go of perfectionism and release extreme self-judgment. They can also help you release lower emotions that interrupt your sense of inner peace so that you learn to see any issue or problem through the lens of love and compassion. Chamuel can surround you in a blanket of warmth and comfort so that you feel safe to move forward fearlessly on your journey.

Gabriel (GAY-bree-ell)

Archangel Gabriel is known to help parents with their children; however, for our purposes this also extends to creative or business endeavors. This angel can boost your visionary power when you are giving birth to new projects. Known as the messenger angel, Gabriel can lend you strength to be creative in life and to share your art and unique message with others. They can also help you become an excellent communicator, so if your work involves any kind of messaging, such as public speaking or writing, Gabriel will support you with all those things and more. This angel can give you the motivation to overcome self-sabotage and help you move past the WBs that usually stall forward progress. In Western magic Gabriel is often associated with the cardinal direction west.

Jophiel (JO-fee-ell)

If you know you lean toward the negative, I know just the angel to help open your eyes to the beauty and opportunity of each moment. Her name is Archangel Jophiel, the angel of beauty. Jophiel can give you a positive perspective shift that doesn't feel forced but rather truly authentic. She's amazing at transforming dark, heavy, negative thoughts into lighter, more optimistic thoughts. So set aside that stinkin' thinkin' and invite Archangel Jophiel to help you see the wonder, hope, and inspiration that always surround you.

Metatron (MEH-tah-trahn)

Archangel Metatron is believed to once have been a human and is said to have brought writing and books to humankind. Reputed to hold the blueprint of all creation, he acts as the bridge between humanity and the Divine. He is said to direct divine energy from Source all the way down to the earth. Metatron guides us all to use our spiritual power for good, to help serve humanity. His main message is "Your divine power is always available to you." In ceremonial magic, he is often associated with the space above us.

Michael (MY-kuhl)

Archangel Michael is a fierce, powerful warrior and protector who can clear negative emotions and fear-based
energy. He has been mentioned in the Bible, the Torah,
and the Koran. The most famous legend of Archangel
Michael is that he defeated Satan. He is the archangel to
call on if you feel you need protection or help putting the
smackdown on your inner demons. He can help you clear
all energy that stops you from pursuing your dreams and
can also help you discover your life purpose. Archangel
Michael is who you want to have in your corner if you are
looking to rise above negativity and step into your next
level of love, joy, and wealth. He represents the cardinal
direction south.

Raphael (rah-fah-ELL)

Archangel Raphael harnesses the divine restorative energy
of Creation to heal humans and all other animals physically, emotionally, and spiritually. He can heal humans at
the soul level and help them erase karmic debts and tackle
addictions. This means he can also be called on to heal
any aspects of self-sabotage that may be interrupting the
path to wealth. Raphael is associated with the east.

Raziel (RAH-zee-ell)

Raziel is known as the grand magician of the archangels
and is the master of esoteric wisdom and the laws of the
universe. He acts as the gatekeeper to the mysteries of
the universe. He governs the veil between the earthly and

spiritual planes and helps humans connect more power-fully with the angelic realm so that prayers and magical intentions can be more clearly communicated. He reigns over all things mystical, mysterious, and metaphysi-cal. Dreams, psychic development, and communication between the material and spiritual worlds are his areas of expertise. He can help you use all your senses to experi-ence divine guidance. Call on Archangel Raziel when you want to gain deep spiritual understanding, boost your magic and psychic abilities, or find unexpected miracles.

Sandalphon (SAN-dahl-fun)

Archangel Sandalphon is known for watching over the earthly realm, gathering the prayers of humans, and carrying them to the Divine Creator. Because of this, Sandalphon is often thought to help with manifesting power, which is quite important for galvanizing your newfound commitment to attracting more wealth and success. He can also give you the endurance and tenac-ity required to make the changes you are being called to make to align your life with more wealth. Sandalphon is depicted as residing below us.

Uriel (YOOR-ee-ell)

Uriel's name means "God's light." He is amazing at increasing smarts and mental clarity, and can light up your mind with brilliant ideas and insights into any query. He's also known for alchemy and can help you turn any-thing, including your intentions to manifest wealth, into gold. Call on Uriel if you need to increase your intellectual capacity, clear your head of mental fog, gain clarity on choices you need to make, or solve a problem. He can help you figure out anything related to your finances or attracting wealth. Ultimately, he can help light the path toward the next steps in manifesting your goals. Uriel represents the north.

Zaphkiel (ZAF-kee-ell)

If you need an angel to help you set strong boundaries, especially with your time and energy, look no further than Archangel Zaphkiel (not to be confused with Archangel Zadkiel, mentioned in my first book, *The Angel Experiment*). They can help you communicate and express your boundaries in a way that will actually allow you to be heard and respected by those around you. They can also help you expand your horizons. If you are afraid to try new things, or have a limited idea about what you're capable of achieving, this archangel can help you open up to the possibilities for growth in your life and open your mind to new frontiers.

Building a Relationship with the Angels through Channel-Writing

When I first started embracing the reality of angels, I didn't learn about them in a book. I just spoke with them as if they were real beings, standing right there with me. I built my relationship with them by casually chatting with them and asking for their help.

Because of this, I always encourage folks like you to put your disbelief aside and simply be open to the notion that angels might be real and be in the room with you now. The simple act of allowing for the possibility that this is true can open doorways of beauty and opportunity for you.

Now, with the understanding that angels just might be right there, waiting to make contact with you, one of my favorite methods of developing a more personal relationship with these beings is a process called channel-writing. Channel-writing is an easy and wonderful method to help you create an authentic connection with specific angels you feel drawn to. The best way to do this is to begin with a powerful practice I call the Quantum Invocation.

The Quantum Invocation is a quick, versatile practice you can use to call on the angels for whatever you may need. You will draw on this technique several times in the coming pages, particularly in chapters 4 and 5, but it will serve you well beyond this book too.

An invocation is similar outwardly to prayer; however, an invocation actually invites the Divine to become alive inside your heart and mind. Not only is the technique fast, but it helps you learn how to truly embody the positive qualities that these angels hold so that, in time, you can actually feel the shift. The Quantum Invocation, when done frequently, can help you pull the weeds in your wealth garden, as well as fertilize the soil so that the new, wealthy thoughts and new, wealthy ways of being can effortlessly emerge from within you.

Before you do the Quantum Invocation, I want you to get into the right mindset for this. I want you to imagine that angels are more than just beings outside you that come to your aid. I want you to also imagine that they are hidden aspects of your own genius and psychology that can be activated and awakened within you. By using the Quantum Invocation technique, you are asking for and giving permission for this aspect of your psyche to come out and play, with the help of the angels.

The Quantum Invocation is easy to do in the mornings, on your breaks, or in the evenings, and once you get the hang of it, it can give you results very quickly.

You can get started with the following steps.

PRACTICE

---- ❧ ----

Quantum Invocation for Channel-Writing

Grab a pen and paper.

Call on God/Source/Creator and Archangel Michael to surround your space with love and protection.

Choose an angel that resonated with you when you read about them earlier in this chapter.

Next, close your eyes and imagine a beautiful nighttime sky above you, full of bright, shining stars. Imagine that those stars represent all the different angels. Say your chosen angel's name three times out loud to help you align with the frequency and vibe of the angel and call them to come to you. Imagine that one of the stars emerges from the limitless space around you, settles gently like a snowflake on the top of your head, and enters your body.

Then imagine the light of that star radiating through your body, breaking up old energy patterns or blockages. Imagine, sense, or feel this light filling your body. Allow it to even radiate out of your pores and then spill into the space around you. Let yourself feel, see, sense, imagine, or know when this process is complete. It shouldn't take more than five to ten minutes.

After you have felt the angel's energy emanating through your body, do your best to feel, sense, or imagine that the angel is now with you and listening to you.

Next, you can ask a simple question like "What message do you have for me today?" At first, the angelic responses could sound like your own thoughts and feelings, but that's OK. Simply write down any thoughts, feelings, hunches, or sensations that begin stirring inside you after you ask this question. Feel free to ask whichever questions you feel called to ask, including any regarding a specific concern in your life.

Write down everything that emerges, even if it doesn't make sense in the beginning. Sometimes, the communication lines can get clogged, and this process will help open them the more you do it.

When you are done writing, always thank the angel for speaking and let them know that they can go in peace.

It's easy to doubt that angel communication is real at first, but the more you practice it, the more you will be able to discern when a true connection has been made. You can receive some pretty incredible information doing this simple exercise, even if you are brand-new to it. It will help you learn to build confidence and trust in your own intuition as well.

It's also a good idea to take special notice of any physical sensations that occur during this process. Sometimes angels and other spiritual allies will show us signals when they are present, and each angel can have a different signal. On occasion you can get the tingles, feel cool air or heat, or get a feeling of peace or comfort. Just notice these things along the way, as this helps you become more sensitive to and aware of when an angel is around.

You can call on multiple angels if you like, but at the beginning, I recommend just getting a feel for one at a time. You can work with the same angel for a few days and then move to another. This can be an amazing daily practice, and many people develop personal relationships with the angels by doing it.

I should also mention that you should use discernment when working with angels or any spiritual force. True angelic voices generally give us hope, a sense of possibility, comfort, and feelings of positivity. Angelic voices are never punishing or negative. If you happen to run into a punishing or negative voice, it usually belongs to one of your inner demons. Pay them no mind and keep attuning your mind to the positive voice. You can also ask the angel to speak to you more loudly and clearly if you are not sensing anything. Practicing this exercise over and over again can really help you create a true kinship with the angels. It's such a wonderful feeling, and it's a wonderful way for the angels to show you that you are not alone and that you have so much love and support surrounding you.

Now that you have the skinny on the angels and allies, it's time to do a little inner investigation. Are you curious about the weeds that might be taking over your inner wealth garden, keeping it from coming to life? Curious about what might be blocking your flow of wealth magic? In the next chapter, you will discover some of your biggest WBs and learn how to pull those dang weeds once and for all. You'll learn an ancient technique called a banishing ritual. A banishing ritual is a quintessential first step of any traditional magical endeavor, and this will help you get ready for your 11-Day Wealth Ritual. You've made the powerful choice to be wealthy through magic, so get ready to roll up your sleeves and get to work!

Chapter 4

Transforming Your Wealth Demons

Can you feel your wealth magic garden starting to sprout? I sure hope so. To prepare you for our 11-Day Wealth Ritual, in the last two chapters I walked you through some steps to get you revved up about being wealthy. You got clear on your intention, and I gave you some simple yet powerful practices to give your ritual a big magnetic boost to help your magical wealth garden flourish. You also met your angelic allies who will help you reach your next level of wealth. For further preparation, we are now going to get into the weeds — the demons that may be threatening your wealth garden.

Have you ever heard the expression "new level, new devil"? What this phrase describes is extremely important when it comes to growing wealth. You best believe that whenever you are making a big change in life, or a bid for more success, love, or power, you can also count on being confronted with new and bigger forms of resistance along the way. Lots of folks run from their goals the moment things get a little hard, and I don't want that to happen to you. Every big uplevel comes with its bigger tests, and I want you to be aware of some of them so that you can outwit the devil standing between you and your beautiful dreams.

As a transformational speaker and leader, I've had the blessing to coach and train CEOs, entrepreneurs, electricians, FBI agents, hairstylists, therapists, stay-at-home parents, and everyone in between. What I've found over the years is that most of them were haunted by and were the puppets of many of the very same dark, sinister forces. Now, you may be thinking that I'm alluding to Satan and his minions, but I'm not. I've discovered forces far more destructive than those guys, and they'll stop at nothing to prevent you from reaching your next level of wealth and success. The forces I'm talking about are your very own bona fide and oh-so-stealthy *inner demons*.

Your inner demons are the ultimate WBs, and they do their best to block your success at just about every turn. They are amazing at projecting dark thoughts and narratives into your mind that tear you down and fill you with self-doubt. Inner demons exploit your pain, your past, and your old financial and personal traumas. They paralyze you with their negativity so that you can't muster the energy to move forward, convincing you that your big dreams are impossible and that you're not capable of doing any better in life. Inner demons are really good at what they do, and it's up to you to learn about them so that you can outwit "the devil" at its own game.

Say Hello to Your Demons

In this chapter, I will introduce you to some of the most dangerous inner demons I have encountered along the way and help you avoid their traps. By becoming conscious of these voices, you can disempower them. Instead of letting those demons stop you, you can nimbly step around them and continue to walk your path toward more success, more wealth, and a more magical life. As George Clinton from the band Funkadelic said, "Free your mind...and your ass will follow." In the case of wealth building, this is also true.

As you explore these inner demons, get a sense of which ones are the most alive for you. You may find that you grapple with most or all of them. If this is the case, please don't be dismayed. The first step in any transformative process is to simply become more self-aware. Knowing that they are there is half the battle — the angels can help you with the rest.

At the end of each section in this chapter, I share some practices, prompts, and specific angels to call on. This will give you a good start at defeating these inner demons. We will also work with these angels and demons a little more deeply later in the book during the eleven-day ritual.

Shame Beast

One of the single most sinister and destructive forces that blocks folks from their next level of wealth and success is a little beastie called shame. Unfortunately, shame is an equal-opportunity demon: I've seen shame effortlessly wreak havoc in my life and in the lives of clients and leaders I serve, encompassing all manner of ages, ethnicities, and countries of origin.

Shame is pervasive and extremely sneaky. It can trick you into believing that you don't like talking in groups; raising your hand; being around people; doing marketing, sales, and public speaking; or, honestly, putting yourself out there and being visible in any way. The Shame Beast may even convince you that you are shy or introverted when the root of this "shyness" is often just shame in disguise.

Shame stops you from being authentic, vulnerable, and visible, and from sharing the truth of who you are. It keeps you playing smaller than you really are and can stop you from stepping more fully into your next level of leadership. Shame makes you compromise who you are and holds the real you hostage.

Can you see how getting trapped by this inner demon could make it particularly difficult for you to make power moves in life toward gaining more wealth? It's challenging to own your power if you are trapped in a shame spiral and secretly apologizing for your very existence.

Oftentimes the shame we experience as adults is greatly influenced by the messages we received as children. We take in those early messages, make assumptions about ourselves and our lives, and write ourselves out of a bigger wealth and success story because of them. Sadly, too many adults believe the voice of the Shame Beast because they've been listening to that voice their whole lives.

I believe the Shame Beast is really the Lord Satan of all the WBs. It lies at the root of many of the weeds that sprout in your wealth garden. Unless shame is addressed and called out for what it is, you will continue to get stuck in the weeds and play shame's game.

Take a moment to feel into the role shame has played or is currently playing in your life. This could be a big one for you, and if it is, I don't want you to miss it. What I love about working with angels is that slowly but surely, they helped me believe in bigger and better things for my life, even though I grappled with the Shame Beast.

Just like they did for me, the angels can help *you* transform this little beastie too. It just might be time to liberate yourself from believing the lies that shame tells you, so that you can be who you came here to be, live the life you envision, and serve others in bigger and broader ways.

So get ready to start kicking shame out of the garden of your life with the practices below.

PRACTICE

— ⚘ —

The Shame Purge Ritual

Do you have a sense that the Shame Beast is playing with you? Here's a little practice to help you loosen its grip.

Grab a piece of paper and writing utensil, close your eyes, sit quietly, and relax through a few cycles of breath.

Let yourself come fully to the present moment. Next, ask shame to show you where it's hiding in your body. Give it a few minutes. You may feel your muscles get tight, tense, cold, hot, heavy, or prickly somewhere. It can manifest in a variety of ways, so give it a few minutes until you get a sense of where shame is showing up for you today physically.

Next, ask yourself the question "What am I really ashamed of?" Allow the answer to begin bubbling up from within you. Do your best not to judge what comes up for you, but write down everything that surfaces. Ask yourself several times, "What am I really ashamed of?" and keep recording thoughts, images, and memories as they arise. By asking over and over again, you may run into even very old memories and events.

Once you have it all written down, create a little shame-burning ceremony for yourself. Find a safe way to burn the memories on the paper. Call on your highest guides and angels, imagine them standing around you, and ask Creator/God/Source and all your divine allies to release you from these feelings. Watch the paper burn, and as it does, imagine that all that stored-up shame energy in your body is burning and that the memories burn with it.

Feel the sense of relief that comes with this ritual, and give gratitude to Creator/Source and your angels for continuing to help release you from the hold of this demon. If you like this ritual, I should mention, you don't have to do this practice only once. You can do it as often as you like for as many days as you like. Especially if you know that shame is a biggie for you.

Angel Ally: To deepen your shame purge, you will want to work with Hahahel, a brilliant source of support who can help you feel stronger on the inside. This kind of inner strength allows you to express yourself more fully by helping you move past and release shame. This angel can give you more confidence and self-esteem so that your self-expression can be more authentic.

"I Suck" Demon

The "I Suck" Demon attacks your confidence from a variety of angles and fills you with a large dose of self-doubt. This demon is deeply rooted in shame, and it constantly talks you out of taking actions in your life that will lead you to more love, more joy, and, yes, more wealth. This little devil is masterful at getting you to consistently devalue your self-worth so that you hide out on the sidelines of life instead of getting into the real game.

You may be familiar with some of the "I Suck" Demon's greatest hits. A few of the songs it sings may even be playing on repeat in your head right now — songs like "I'm not good enough," "I suck with money," "I'm not worthy," "Nobody likes me," and "I don't belong" are some of this demon's faves. Do any of those sound familiar? They are definitely oldies but goodies for those who love to dance with this demon.

When I coach and speak to groups on expanding their wealth capacity and upleveling their businesses and careers and lives, I find that many folks have a fundamental belief that they generally suck or aren't worthy of having more. Sometimes these feelings of not being good enough are a lifelong struggle. Sometimes they come from early childhood, or we might get messages from society that we just don't fit the worthiness bill based on our skin color; our gender, sexual orientation, or gender identity; or another aspect of who we are that makes us unique.

What I have learned from doing angel work is that we all have an amazing power inside us that can dismantle the "I Suck" Demon's stranglehold on our psyches. I believe it's essential that we all look at this demon head-on, not just for ourselves but also to help and inspire others to do the same.

Signs that the "I Suck" Demon may be having its way with you:

- You spend a large part of your day not feeling good enough.
- You feel inferior to others.
- You don't trust yourself and feel like you are somehow gonna mess everything up.
- You constantly tell yourself that you suck, and actually believe it.
- You have a hard time defending yourself when wronged.
- You often believe that other people's feelings are more important than your own.
- You feel guilty charging money for your services or raising your prices.
- A part of you feels like you deserve to be punished.
- When people tell you that you suck, you believe them.

- When people tell you that you rule, you don't believe them.

How's that for a list? Do you see any of the traits I've listed in yourself? If so, I'm excited for you, because I know that today is the day you start letting that demon go.

You can begin by doing the practice I've given you below.

PRACTICE

—————————— ✤ ——————————

Owning Your Badassery

Work through the following in your grimoire.

Sit quietly, and make a list of all the thoughts you have that make you feel unworthy of more wealth. Then write down the opposite of each of those thoughts. For instance, if you write down "I'm not smart enough," next to it you can write down something like "I'm a genius."

Next, you will work with your breath to do some angel healing. First, take a moment, center yourself, call in your guides and angels, and ask your angels to release you from the negative thoughts and feelings you wrote down. You can even imagine angels coming into the room and taking them from you. As you exhale, imagine you are breathing out all the negative thoughts. Feel the angels taking these dark thoughts and feelings from you. Now ask the angels to help you feel and believe the positive statements you wrote down. As you inhale, imagine Creator/God/Source and the angels filling you up with all the good thoughts and feelings you wrote down.

Wait until you feel even the slightest shift in your body. Sometimes folks can feel a little lighter, or more peaceful, or more relaxed. Once you get a sense that something has shifted inside you, you are ready to party.

Feel free to make a copy of the positive statements from your grimoire to add to your wealth altar and ask the angels to keep helping you embody these new principles. You can also use the positive statements you wrote down as daily affirmations to remind yourself of what a badass you really are. If you are looking for some amazing wealth-affirmation inspiration, you can go to my website at AngelWealthMagic.com/Resources. There are hundreds of wealth affirmations for you to choose from there.

Angel Ally: When combating the "I Suck" Demon (and the Shame Beast too), Pedahiel can help you. Actually, this one angel can support you with so many of the inner demons. Pedahiel can imbue you with the quality of grandeur. This quality may seem arrogant at first, but with Pedahiel's assistance, you'll soon feel truly *worthy* of it and *good enough* to receive all life has to offer. They can help you appreciate yourself and feel appreciated by others. If you need to be held in higher regard in your circle, this angel can help you respect yourself and be more respected by friends, family, and colleagues; your boss, fans, and clients; loan officers; and anyone else.

Impostor Demon

The Impostor Demon is closely connected with the Shame Beast and the "I Suck" Demon but deserves a mention all its own. It's estimated that 70 percent of people struggle with the Impostor Demon, or impostor syndrome, and — get this — the folks who struggle with the Impostor Demon the most are often very high achievers.

This tricky demon makes you feel like you are faking it in your work and worry that eventually "they" will find out you are a fraud, charlatan, liar, cheater, or phony, and are unqualified or incompetent. These thoughts and feelings can arise when you have done nothing wrong. This demon constantly makes you doubt your abilities, your skill set, your accomplishments, and your life experience, even when you are truly an expert in your field.

I have worked with purpose-driven, successful folks who have had lifelong struggles with this demon. The Impostor Demon can make you believe that you aren't ready for that next big power move in life. It will stop you from things like submitting your résumé for a next-level job, asking for a raise or promotion, starting that Etsy shop, or getting funding for that new company you want to build, because you feel like you don't really know what you are doing, even when you really do.

Let's say you have dreams of becoming the next big inspirational speaker, but you struggle with depression. Due to this demon, you could stop yourself from pursuing that dream because you might feel like a fraud. Or maybe you want to be a leading relationship expert, but you are on your third divorce. This demon can trick you into believing that your relationships need to be 100 percent on point in order for you to be qualified to help others, when the truth is that being a human with real human problems doesn't diminish your expertise. If anything, it makes you more relatable.

As you can see, the Impostor Demon is amazing at throwing up smoke and mirrors to get you to stay in the "safe zone." And, well, the "safe zone" is a nice place to visit, but it's not a place to stay if you want to build long-term, sustainable wealth. So, if the Impostor Demon is currently punking you, don't let it. It's just trying to talk you down from being your fully amazing self. You have just as much right as anyone else to share who you are, your gifts, and your message.

So, say it with me: "I belong here, I have the right to be here, and I have something special to share!" And if you are ready to banish the Impostor Demon and begin claiming more of your awesomeness, you can start working with the practices below.

PRACTICE

Kicking the Impostor Demon to the Curb

Work through the following in your grimoire.

Call on your angels, sit, and let yourself feel into where it is in your life that you still feel like an impostor. Write that down.

What are the thoughts you consistently have that

make you feel like an impostor? Ask the angels to help you let go of those thoughts and embrace your gifts and value.

Next, write about your many accomplishments and how valuable and resourceful you are. Write down all the reasons why you deserve to be loved, respected, and cared for. Allow your heart to tell you why you have the right to shine and to be wealthy. Write about all the ways in which you are *not* an impostor. Let yourself really feel the blessings and gifts that you bring to the table already. If there is one thing the angels have shown me, it is that each and every human has a very special medicine inside them that is beautiful and unique, and supports others. That includes you, so it's time to own it.

Refer back to this writing frequently to remind yourself of how awesome you are.

Angel Ally: The angel for this one is Vehuiah. Vehuiah can help you move past the fear of rejection and give you an overall boost of courage to take your leadership to the next level. They can help you build the confidence to share your work, put yourself out there, and shamelessly offer your services.

Self-Sabotage Demon

The Self-Sabotage Demon does an incredible job of undermining your goals and broader vision for your life. If you have ever had a big, inspired dream only to lose interest right before the finish line, then you have met this demon.

This is personally one of my biggest foes, so if you are a self-saboteur, I feel your pain. The Self-Sabotage Demon makes you engage in behaviors that lower your self-esteem, distract you, and stop your progress just before you reach your destination.

The Self-Sabotage Demon can show up in your life in several creative ways, and it's up to you to be able to see it for what it is. Procrastination, maintaining poor boundaries, staying in a toxic relationship, time mismanagement, fear of commitment, excessive personal drama, and even addiction can all be signs that the Self-Sabotage Demon may be close by.

Besides the more obvious symptoms that I've listed above, this demon's effects can sometimes be more subtle and unconscious. This demon can infiltrate your mind and show up as the consistently negative thoughts and judgments that you hold about yourself, your life, or your future. Having excessive negative thoughts will demotivate and distract you from taking the sacred actions you are guided to take to help heal your life — and your bank account.

If the Self-Sabotage Demon is a biggie for you, no need to punish yourself over it. I've never met a human who wasn't working with this demon in one way or another. We are humans, after all. Your task now is to simply become conscious of the ways this creative demon may be playing their game with you, since it's usually pretty good at hiding in plain sight. Once you can see self-sabotage clearly, it gets so much easier to release it — and easier to pull the weeds caused by this WB from your wealth garden.

If you are a master self-saboteur, then we have a practice you can begin with to help neutralize this demon.

PRACTICE

Self-Sabotage No Más!

Answer the following questions in your grimoire:

- In what ways do I sabotage myself from having more in life?
- How have I sabotaged myself in the past from being wealthier?
- How am I sabotaging myself right now from being wealthier?
- What thoughts do I consistently think that might be blocking me from more wealth and success?

Take an inventory of your current behaviors, daily habits, and repetitive thoughts that don't align with or support your wealth goals. Make a full list. Then ask yourself, "What am I willing to change in order to be wealthier?" Let the ideas flow, and write everything down. Review what you wrote, and commit to changing at least one thing in order to become wealthier.

The goal of this exercise is to help you be honest about what you are doing so that you can become more conscious of your patterns and make the conscious *choice* to change some of those behaviors.

To take this practice to the next level, you can also write a letter to the angels asking them to release you from these behaviors and to replace them with thoughts and actions that align with your next level of wealth.

Angel Ally: Raduriel is an angel of creativity who can stop you from self-sabotage and raise your vibe. They can give you a boost of enthusiasm and infuse you with the energy of inspiration, passion, and creativity so that you move past the doldrums and the self-loathing and "sing your song" to the world.

Confusion Demon

The Confusion Demon is a sneaky WB indeed. Also known as the Demon of Indecision, it is closely linked to an inability to make powerful choices with conviction. And I've already told you about how important choice making is in the game of wealth manifesting and magic.

The Confusion Demon works by stopping your soul-aligned and inspired action in its tracks, making you afraid that you are going to arrive at a wrong or bad decision. Sometimes this demon can cause you to obsess over this choice so that forward progress gets delayed by weeks, months, or even *years*.

This demon is also strongly linked with the fear of commitment. If you don't like committing and shrink from a higher level of responsibility, this demon will exploit that fear to the point where you eventually choose nothing and walk away from the idea and dream before it even gets going.

For example, when I'm speaking to new entrepreneurs, they can easily get stuck on the most basic of choices, something as simple as deciding on their title: owner, CEO, or Grand Pooh-Bah. Some people can get so lost in making this fundamental choice that their inspiration and momentum wane — all because of one teensy thing that they are too afraid to get wrong. Decisions like which software to use, who to hire, where to invest, or what kind of font to use can all greatly slow down your wealth progress if you let this demon win. The Confusion Demon can distort the magnitude of decisions like these and make them almost feel like they are a matter of life and death. Of course, these *can* be key decisions as you are actively pursuing growing wealth, but this demon amplifies the importance so much that sometimes people back away from making a choice altogether.

If you are someone who gets confused or struggles a lot with indecision, then this demon needs to be seen for what it is. It's simply a distraction designed to slow or stop your progress.

One thing I have learned in addressing this demon is that you must first realize that making a choice, any choice, is better than staying in stagnation for another two weeks, two months, or two years. Spirit rewards folks in motion. So if you catch yourself getting stuck on one decision for too long, just make the dang decision. Flip a coin if you have to, and don't worry too much that it's the "wrong" choice, because, whatever it is, you can always make adjustments and course corrections along the way to help you realign with your goals.

Don't let the Confusion Demon win. Commit to moving forward by making a decision, even if you aren't 100 percent sure that the decision you are making is the "perfect" one. Clarity doesn't come from overthinking things. True clarity comes from taking action and making adjustments along the way.

If you struggle with feeling confused a lot, you can start shifting this demon with the practice below.

PRACTICE

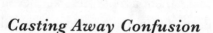

Casting Away Confusion

Work on the following prompts in your grimoire:

- Do you find yourself saying "I don't know" a lot? If so, how does saying "I don't know" protect you?
- Do you struggle with making commitments? What's the worst thing that happens when you commit?
- How is confusion stopping your progress in life right now? What choice needs to be made to move the needle more toward your rockstar life?

Angel Ally: The angel Daniel can help you with gaining clarity and making amazing choices. If you get confused and have a hard time with small or big decisions, be sure to connect with Daniel! This angel can give you confidence in your decisions and can help you reduce the anxiety or heavier emotions that you might be carrying along the way.

Perfection Demon

Like the Confusion Demon, the Perfection Demon loves to stop you in your tracks and delay your forward progress so that you never quite feel ready to make a power move in the direction of your big wealth dreams.

Here are some questions for you that relate to this demon:

- Do you hold yourself to excessively high standards?
- Do you have an all-or-nothing mentality?
- Are you rarely satisfied with the work you do?
- Does it take you a long time to finish things because you want them to be flawless?
- Are you highly critical of yourself, even when others have told you that you have done a good job?
- Do you feel that in order to get things done right, you have to do them all yourself?

Any of this sound familiar? Believe it or not, perfectionism can greatly slow your progress toward a big uplevel and can hypnotize you into believing that you have to jump through an endless number of hoops before you can get to your dream.

This demon wants you to work way harder than necessary, putting up roadblocks to success. Let's say you have been dreaming of becoming a badass, successful healer; this demon might tell you that you need to earn ten more certifications before you can put yourself out there. But usually, this is just a ruse to slow you down.

This demon can also make you feel like you are lost in a maze of details that you need to execute perfectly before you finally look for that new job, start marketing yourself, or even get your new business running. So, instead of helping you take strategic shortcuts, this demon can make you take excessive longcuts.

If you lean too heavily toward perfectionism, it could take you years to finally feel like you are truly ready to make the moves you want to make toward more freedom, love, and wealth. What the Perfection Demon doesn't want you to know is that *right now* is the perfect moment to start taking action to make your dreams come true. This demon also doesn't want you to know that creating something that's a little ugly and imperfect is better than creating nothing at all.

You may have been there or know someone who has. You want to start a new business but become so bogged down in getting your website just right or spend so much time obsessing about the color palette and branding that nearly a year goes by before you get your first client. Without this demon sitting on your shoulder, you might approach things differently, realize that time is money, and elicit the help of others with the details. You'll have a sense of when things are "good enough" and be able to get things off the ground and score your first client in one-tenth of the time, without worrying about everything being perfect.

Believing in the perfect anything will rob you of your precious time, and too much time spent pursuing perfect outcomes can deeply undercut the bottom line. So instead of waiting for the perfect state of affairs to arrive, keep moving forward and allow yourself to take perfectly imperfect steps toward your bigger dreams. This will expedite your progress and your success.

If you need help vanquishing the Perfection Demon, you can start with the practices below.

PRACTICE

— ⚜ —

Perfecting Imperfection

Work out answers to the following in your grimoire:

- How has perfectionism affected your life?
- How might perfectionism be slowing your progress right now?
- Whom did you learn your perfectionism from?
- What is the worst thing that happens if you aren't perfect?
- What is the best thing that happens if you aren't perfect?
- What are you putting off right now by waiting for the perfect moment?
- What can you commit to doing today to help move incrementally forward?

Angel Ally: Archangel Chamuel can help you let go of perfectionism by releasing extreme self-judgment and dissolving the lower emotions that drive the need for perfectionism. This angel can help you find inner peace so that you learn to see any imagined issue or problem with new eyes. Chamuel can support you in feeling safe to move forward with flexibility and courage that springs from the heart.

PRACTICE

❧

Quantum Invocation for Banishing Your Demons

I am super excited to now share one of my favorite tactics for disempowering these demons so that you can more easily open the path to more wealth. It's another version of the Quantum Invocation technique you learned in the last chapter. This time you'll use it to quickly neutralize the voices of the inner demons (or the WBs) that may be blocking your road to wealth. Here's how to do it.

Look back through the list of inner demons and choose the one that is bugging you the most right now. Next, choose an angel that directly addresses the inner demon you would like to neutralize.

Now, close your eyes and imagine a beautiful night sky surrounding you, full of bright, shining stars. Imagine that those stars represent all the different angels. Say your chosen angel's name three times out loud to help you align with the frequency and vibe of the angel and call them to come to you. Imagine that one of the stars emerges from the limitless space around you, settles gently like a snow-flake on the top of your head, and enters your body. Let that star settle in your belly, in your heart, or wherever it feels best to you.

Then imagine the light of that star radiating through your body, breaking up old energy patterns or dark webs that represent the inner demon. Imagine, sense, or feel this light filling your body. Allow it to even radiate out of your pores and then spill into the space around you. Let yourself feel, see, sense, or know when this process is complete. It shouldn't take more than five to ten minutes.

Ask the angel to help you embody whatever it is that you would like to feel by calling on the angel. For example, if I wanted to work with Vehuiah to help me banish the demon of confusion and embody more willpower, I would say something like "Vehuiah, Vehuiah, Vehuiah, I ask you to help me become a master of willpower. Help my words match my actions and help me keep my commitments without delay. Thank you."

Remember and affirm the qualities you are choosing to activate inside you. For example, if you are calling on Lauviah for confidence, hold this intention until the light that's getting activated inside you fills your body with confidence and dissolves any feelings of self-doubt.

Notice how your body feels after this invocation. Note any shifts that you experience in your magical grimoire, and if you have time, take a moment to record any intuitive messages you might receive. Intuitive work is so subtle in the beginning, so even if you feel like you might be making something up, write it down anyway.

——————— ✤ ———————

I hope this chapter has opened your eyes to how these demons might be infiltrating your inner wealth garden. As I've mentioned before, half the battle is just knowing that they are there.

The angels want you to know that the only limitation you have is in your own mind. It's time to open your eyes, heart, and mind to the possibility that behind these apparent gatekeepers, something extraordinary is waiting for you.

Allow your process with the angels to unfold as if you are unraveling a great mystery. Allow the angels to reignite your passion and your purpose, and they will reveal the golden path of awesomeness that awaits you.

In the next chapter, I go over some mindset tricks and traits that self-made wealthy folks seem to have in common. These traits can make or break your sustainable wealth game, so I wanted to be sure to share them with you. Get ready for the angels to help you learn how to embody these qualities and kick-start the wealthy, magical lifestyle of your dreams.

Let's keep this wealth magic party going, shall we?

Chapter 5

Magical Mindset Tricks
of the Wealthy

Now that I've talked to you about how the little WB devils may be standing in the way of your wealthy lifestyle, I want to share some magical mindset tips that can expedite your wealth manifestations and help your inner wealth garden flourish.

Throughout my own magical wealth-building journey, I have met, coached, trained, and spoken in front of some pretty amazing, magical, and highly successful humans. These are people who walk in both the spiritual world and the world of entrepreneurship and who have amassed millions of dollars doing heart-centered work. I find that people who have a strong connection to Spirit and have learned how to make an amazing living offering a service to the world are incredible role models for the kind of wealth we are working toward on this journey.

I am excited to share a few of the key habits and

mindset tricks of these amazing folks so that you can begin hiring the angels to help you embody these qualities yourself. A wealth-and-success mindset sometimes doesn't come to most of us naturally, so please don't be hard on yourself if you find that you struggle with most of these. The angels put this book into your hands because it's time for you to make the shift, and as we have discussed before, there's no better time than the present.

In each section below, I include a combination of grimoire prompts, exercises, and even specific angels that can help you embody these new ways of thinking and being. As with the last chapter, as you read through these sections, take a long, hard, honest look at how you are doing in each category. Assess your mastery of each, and if you need to enhance some of these qualities in yourself, you can start by working the practices I've provided for you.

The Love of Money, Honey

Self-made millionaires, even the heart-centered, spiritual ones, have learned to love money and have let go of negative feelings and conditioning around it. They've stopped telling themselves that money is evil or only for greedy people and have embraced the reality that money is an amazing tool that can be used to serve their families, their communities, and even the world.

So the question is, how do you feel about money — greenbacks, cashola, cabbage, coin? And I mean, *really* feel about it? Do you resent money? Do you secretly think that cashola is evil? Do you hate cabbage? Does coin make you nervous? Do you think that only greedy or bad people have a lot of cash? Do you resent rich people?

Check in with yourself about it real quick. If you want to know how you really feel about money, try this: Sit quietly for thirty seconds and let yourself think about money and your financial situation. Think about the money in your bank account, your bills, and your credit cards. Notice what happens to your body and your emotions when you do. When people do this brief check-in with themselves, some immediately feel their heart begin to race or experience nervousness in their belly or heaviness on their chest. Sometimes they even break out into a sweat! I know I used to.

So did you feel excited about money? Or did it make you a little anxious, frustrated, or angry? If you don't feel all good about money, then it's time to give your relationship with it a little love. Money is energy and responds to the energy that you put out toward it. If you spend a lot of time consciously or unconsciously sending a stink vibe toward it, then you may accidentally be repelling instead of attracting it. It's much like wooing a new lover. When wooing a new lover, would you write a dating profile that looked like this?

Hi, I'm Billy and I hate dating. Dating never works out for me because I really suck at it, plus I'm not really worthy of love. For fun, I like to spend my time sulking, punching myself in the head, and taking long strolls down Butthurt Alley.

P.S. I don't believe in love, I'm especially heinous in bed, and I hate you already. Hit me up.

Doesn't Billy sound like a tasty treat? Not really. Just like Billy would repel a new lover with his not-so-hot profile, if your thoughts are full of negativity about money, you will end up pushing money away instead of attracting it.

If any of this negativity around money resonates with you, it's time for a mindset shift. I want you to begin thinking of money more like a new lover than a foe. Keep an open mind and have curiosity about it. Make the choice to shift your attitude toward money. Take the time to really get to know it and to understand how the energy behind money works.

The following practice has helped me and many of my clients detox their relationship with money and re-create a healthy mindset around it. This healthier mindset will bring you one serious step closer to your wealthy lifestyle.

PRACTICE

Chatting with the Spirit of Money

This technique is rooted in Gestalt psychology and can help you quickly discover your WBs so that you can rebuild a healthy relationship with money.

Take a moment to first write out all your negative thoughts and feelings about money on a sheet of paper.

Pull out your wallet and place it opposite you on a table or on a chair next to you. Your wallet is going to represent the spirit of money.

Invite the spirit of money to come and have a chat

with you as if you are enjoying a cup of coffee or tea together.

You are going to ask money a series of questions. In between the questions, you will listen and feel with your inner ears for the answers that money gives you. Trust the information that comes to you.

Next, you can ask money questions like the following. Feel free to change the questions or use questions of your own. I'm simply offering you a guidepost to get you started:

- Money, why do you make me feel this way?
- Why don't I have more of you?
- How can I make and attract more of you?
- How can I have a better relationship with you?

Ask any other questions you may have. After each, make sure to listen closely and trust the information you receive; then write down the answer.

At the end of this process, thank money for the information. Thank it for all the support it's already given you in life, and let it know you are ready to receive a whole heck of a lot more of it.

Reflect on and write down what you discovered during your meeting with the spirit of money. Based on your conversation, write down one specific action step you can take to begin healing your relationship with money.

What most people discover when they do this exercise is that the spirit of money is quite friendly and kind. They also discover that money is fairly neutral and isn't "out to get" them the way they thought it was. They realize that their money situation is simply a result of their dominant thoughts about it.

If you know that your relationship with money needs a lot of work, I recommend that you keep doing this exercise frequently until you love the spirit of money and feel like money has become a true ally. Remember, if you love money, money will love you back. Say it with me now: "I love money and money loves me." Keep saying it until you can feel the truth of it, and watch money begin to flow to you in magical ways.

Angel Ally: If you desire more help in deepening your love for money, you can do a Quantum Invocation with angel Nememiah. Nememiah can help you open the flow of financial riches and also let go of your fears and worries about money. (If you forgot how to do the Quantum Invocation, you can review the steps in chapter 3.)

Über-Audacity

Have you ever had a big dream? Well, one of the major differences between self-made wealthy folks and the average human is that they don't simply have big dreams. They also have the audacity to take action steps to turn those dreams into reality.

Audacity means being willing to take bold risks to make your amazing dreams happen. Many folks want to uplevel their wealth, yet they aren't really willing to take the risks to get there. Self-made millionaires know that wealth making is not a spectator sport and that you have to put some skin in the game if you want to go big.

Being audacious and taking bold risks also implies that you have to be willing on some level to get it wrong, to fail, and to have a healthy splatter of egg on your face if the vision flops. It takes serious audacity to move in the direction of more love, more joy, and more wealth, because when you make power moves in life, you have no guarantees that things will work out.

Being audacious also means being willing to make some sacrifices along the way to free up space for your big dream. Sometimes, you'll need to sacrifice things like your time and money in order to make big things happen. Self-made wealthy folk view sacrifices like these not as sacrifices at all. They know that these "sacrifices" are really investments in their future, with the potential for some pretty amazing returns. And if you want to shift into a wealthy mindset, you will need to make those investments in your dreams too.

In the beginning, making these kinds of investments can feel like a serious risk. I know this firsthand. When my kids were very young, the angels began inspiring me to step out of the box and expand my career from being solely a psychotherapist to becoming an international transformational leader. This was a big, scary, but also exciting vision, and I knew nothing about taking off in this direction.

I also didn't know how to start my own international business, so I reluctantly decided to hire a business coach. I actually cried when I did because it cost a lot more than I felt like I could afford. Another part of me felt that hiring a business coach would be a huge waste of time, because

I thought I would probably drop the ball (hello, Shame Beast and "I Suck" Demon). I felt so selfish and guilty for taking that money away from my family because it felt like a huge gamble (same demons again). But I decided to take the risk and made the audacious move to go through with it anyway.

The coaching did, in fact, fail for the first five months. I hadn't made a dollar because I was jumping all over the place with my ideas and what I wanted to create (Confusion Demon). So then my coach sat me down and said, "You only have one month left. It's time for you to choose your offering [defeat the Confusion Demon] and send an email to your people inviting them to whatever you are offering." I deeply desired to offer a six-month intuitive healing training but felt paralyzed by the idea, because I wasn't sure that I could pull it off (Impostor Demon). I hated my coach for making me do this. It was terrifying for me because just about every bone in my body knew that it would fail ("I Suck" Demon). So I prayed deeply, did some angel rituals, and mustered the audacity to send that damn email.

Sweat beading on my brow, I managed to click the "send" button, and within seventy-two hours of sending that one email I doubled my annual income. Folks actually signed up! It was exciting and perplexing all at once. It was the first financial miracle I experienced by working with some of the very principles that I'm teaching you in this book, and it was earth-shattering...in a good way. It shattered everything that I thought was possible for myself and my life. And it happened because I had finally mustered the audacity to quit listening to my inner demons and take action on my dream, even when my inner demons were doing their best to stop me. Clicking the "send" button was a special kind of torture, but *I did it anyway*.

The important point to remember is that the angels can drop down amazing inspiration for you to create your next level of wealth, but the rest is your job. They can't do all the heavy lifting for you by themselves. When you are going for the big wealth uplevel, you also may have to take some terrifying steps to turn that vision into a reality. So when you are taking action to make your big dream happen and you feel the terror building up, don't run. Be audacious. Do the thing anyway. Keep going, even if you break out in a sweat from the fear. Who knows, there could be a miracle waiting for you on the other side of that terror.

Now, I want to ask you, on a scale of 1 to 10, how audacious are you? How willing are you to take positive risks to pursue your dreams? Do you have the audacity to actually believe in and execute your dream, even if it feels like a gamble and you aren't sure it will work out?

If you don't, it's OK. The following grimoire work and angel-ally suggestions should help get you started.

PRACTICE

Rocking Your Audacity

Reflect on these questions and write your responses in your grimoire:

- What is your big wealth dream?
- What are you willing to risk to make this dream become a reality?
- What sacrifices or investments are you willing to make for the sake of this dream?
- What's the worst thing that can happen if you pursue your dream and it doesn't work out the way you want it to?
- What's the best thing that can happen if you summon the audacity, you make the sacrifices, and it actually *does* work out? Let your body feel the outcome of this awesomeness.
- What is one audacious action step that will help you move the needle on turning your wealth dream into a reality? Commit to taking that action this week. Ask this question at least weekly, if not daily.

Angel Ally: Try out a Quantum Invocation with angel Hayiel, who can help you muster the audacity and strength to turn your dreams into reality. They can help give you the focus to take action on your dreams and audaciously offer your next level of service to the world.

True Optimism

When you think about your life and your future, do you mostly have negative thoughts or positive thoughts? Do you lean toward being a hopeful, optimistic person? Or do you tend toward more pessimism and doom and gloom?

A fixed negative mindset can be a huge roadblock on

your journey to creating long-term sustainable wealth. The successful folks I've met along the way are often truly optimistic. Now, by "truly optimistic," I don't mean that they believe that only good things will ever happen for them. They aren't delusional, nor do they avoid their darker feelings when things get rough. They are usually pretty grounded in reality, meaning they are aware of their shadows, their fears, their doubts, and the possibility that their next projects may fail.

What makes these successful people truly optimistic is that when life throws them lemons, they work with the lemons, they get curious about the lemons, they ask the lemons questions, they learn from the lemons, and they know that when things do get rough, it's temporary. They know that they will eventually develop a strategy to make lemonade out of those lemons.

I had my own sour lemon experience before I sent that email that doubled my annual salary. About 96 percent of me was convinced that this email would flop and that nobody would respond. But the other 4 percent of me felt differently. It was excited about it. That 4 percent was thinking, *What if this actually does work? Wouldn't it be amazing?* The answer was, of course, yes. So with the help of the angels, I was able to lean into that 4 percent of honest optimism and hit "send."

I want you to know that in order to make amazing things happen, you don't have to pretend to feel 100 percent on board. You don't have to "fake it 'til you make it." All you need in the beginning is to simply be able to hear just a little of the authentically optimistic voice inside you.

If you learn how to listen to that voice instead of the hostile one, that tiny, beautiful voice just might lead you to a life beyond your wildest dreams.

If you struggle with seeing the positive in your life or your future or remaining positive in the face of adversity, this one mindset shift can make all the difference for you on your wealth-making adventure. And please don't fret if this one doesn't come naturally to you. The angels really can help. Your first step is to make the choice to be more optimistic and ask for assistance.

PRACTICE

---- ✤ ----

Optimism Uptick

Work through the following in your grimoire:

- Where do you fall on the optimism scale, from 1 to 10?
- If you lean toward the negative, where did you learn that from? Whom did you learn that from?
- What do you need to do to become a 10 on the optimism scale?

Angel Ally: If you lean toward the negative, I know just the angel to help you open your eyes to the beauty, hope, and opportunity of each moment. Her name is Archangel Jophiel, the angel of beauty. So set aside your negativity, and invite her in. After you do your Quantum Invocation with Archangel Jophiel, try the following additional step to attune your mind to a truly optimistic outlook: Look around you and say out loud, "I see beauty in everything that surrounds me." For just a few minutes, allow yourself to open up to the perfection and beauty of the moment. Let yourself contemplate the beauty in your life and in all things: your relationships, your home, your career, your future, and even your bank account.

Jophiel can work extra fast for you, so if you do these steps, pay attention to any positive shifts in your overall outlook on life. Make sure to thank her if you notice any level of improvement.

Beautiful and optimistic mind, here we come!

The Tenacity of a Honey Badger

Do you tend to give up when things get hard? Well, if you are looking to attract long-term sustainable wealth, and not just quick cash, you'll need a wee bit more tenacity. Tenacity means having the mental strength to resist opposition, danger, or hardship.

Self-made wealthy folks never stop believing and dreaming, even in the face of adversity. They see an apparent obstacle and aren't afraid to attack it head-on, sometimes over and over again, until they have a breakthrough. Kind of like a honey badger.

Have you ever seen honey badger vs. lion videos? A little honey badger will attack and charge a pride of lions even though the lions are ginormous by comparison. The honey badger keeps attacking and attacking, until eventually the lions walk away because the smaller critter wears them out. Now that's serious tenacity.

Most animals (including humans) would see a pride of lions on their path and run to the hills for safety. Not the honey badger. Honey badgers don't run away from challenges; they run toward them and don't stop until they get what they want. They are like the undefeated UFC champions of the animal kingdom.

Because of their fierce tenacity, honey badgers even have some memes flying around social media that read "Honey Badgers Don't Care" and my personal fave, "Honey Badgers Don't Give a Sh*t." Like the honey badger, self-made millionaires don't care either. They don't care if they stumble a little here and there, because they have thick skin and are up for the challenge. They understand that apparent failure doesn't mean the vision is lost; it simply means that the strategy needs to be adjusted. They learn from their losses, pick themselves up, dust themselves off, and get back to it with their special brand of honey badger jiujitsu.

So if you are executing your divine vision and you hit a snag, catch a little resistance, or run into a hater or two, don't let it stop you. Learn from the great tenacity of the honey badger and put up a fight. You picked up this book for a reason: something inside you is inspiring you to rise up and claim more financial power for yourself. Can you feel it? Because that feeling is definitely worth fighting for — over and over again. As Oprah Winfrey once said, "Do the one thing you think you cannot do. Fail at it. Try again. Do better the second time. The only people who never tumble are those who never mount the high wire. This is your moment. Own it."

A little tenacity can go a very long way on your awesome wealth-making journey, so if you need some help with this, you can start with the practice below.

PRACTICE

——————— ✧ ———————

Dreamin' Like a Honey Badger

Work through the following in your grimoire:

- On a scale of 1 to 10, rate how tenacious you are when it comes to pursuing your dreams. Brainstorm some tools, practices, and behaviors that could help you get to 10.
- Write a love letter to your big dream, committing to the process of making it happen…no matter what. The letter can start: "Dear Big Dream, I vow to …" Let yourself feel the emotion of this, as if you deeply mean it.

Angel Ally: If you need a further boost in the tenacity department, the archangel Sandalphon can help you finish what you start. They can give you the persistence, resilience, and energy to keep going and carry out your vision. Perform a Quantum Invocation with Sandalphon if you want to rock some serious tenacity and manifest your big dream.

Just Sayin' No

Another mindset shift that self-made millionaires embody is the ability to set strong boundaries around their time and energy. They've learned how to say the word *no* to others without compromise. The truth is that your next level of wealth will require you to implement your next level of boundaries.

When you work with angels on the daily, eventually you will come to the realization that you and your time are extremely valuable. I'm hoping you know that already, but if you don't yet, it's true. In order to make power moves in your life, it's essential that you quit dumping time and energy into people, places, and things that don't fill you up. You have a limited amount of time and energy, which is why it's extra important to be more judicious about how, when, and with whom you share these vital resources.

Self-made wealthy folks understand that setting boundaries with respect to their time and energy is an act of self-love. They also know that it is one of the biggest keys to their success. Being willing to say no to the activities, people, and behaviors that don't align with your big vision and who you truly are will give you more time and energy to say yes to your beautiful dreams.

Some questions to answer in the beginning are:

- Do you have difficulty finding alone time for yourself?
- Is your schedule full of things that you really don't want to do but that you do to be nice or out of guilt?

- Do you have a hard time saying no to the requests of friends, family, or colleagues?
- Do you spend too much time on social media?
- Do you dedicate a lot of your time to volunteering for things that you don't really enjoy but do out of guilt or obligation?
- Do you put other people's needs before your own?

If you answered "yes" to most of those, it's time to make this mindset shift.

You can't be a true leader in your life if you are constantly reacting to the needs of other people. To build sustainable wealth, you must be proactive, not reactive, about your time. You will need a significant amount of solo time to help your heart, mind, soul, body, and life stay balanced. This will give you space to dream the big dream, boost your creativity, commune with Spirit, do research, get coaching, and take those amazing action steps you are being called to take.

Remember, being a big martyr kills your big dreams. So, leave the martyrdom to Jesus, and learn to say "No!" more to others, so that you can say "Yes!" more to your big, tasty, wealthy vision. It may feel weird in the beginning, but you'll get used to it and will be grateful for the extra party time you've set aside for yourself and for your dreams.

If you struggle with setting strong boundaries and valuing your personal time, we have some help for you.

PRACTICE

—— ✤ ——

Building Better Boundaries

Work through the following in your grimoire:

- How much time do you allot during the week for your own creative and personal time? Take an honest inventory of how you spend your time.
- What are the activities that you would love to stop doing?
- What would you love to do more of?
- If you could wave a magic wand, what would the ideal weekday look like for you?
- What is one action step you can take now to begin making this change happen?

Angel Ally: A Quantum Invocation with Archangel Zaphkiel can help you set strong boundaries with your time and energy. Consider this angel like a sentinel guarding and watching over the perimeter of your castle. They can help you protect your home, your work, your time, and your energy. They can also help you communicate your boundaries in a way that will make people actually hear you and respect you.

Good Company

Before I end this chapter, I want to mention a few extra things you can do to help anchor into your awesome wealth magic mindset.

Have you ever heard the Jim Rohn quote "You are the average of the five people you spend the most time with"? Well, I've found this to be true. If you are around a lot of negative people or folks who embrace the status quo, that mindset does the opposite of inspiring you to have big dreams and big wealth breakthroughs.

If you want to achieve amazing success in life and take your wealth and leadership to the next level, it helps to surround yourself with others who have done or are doing those things. One of the biggest problems people have with this is that they don't know many wealthy or successful folks. I know I didn't for the majority of my life, so if this is the case for you, I've got your back. I have some great strategies to help you learn from and get inspired by the wealthy, whether you know any millionaires in your immediate circle or not.

First, if you do happen to know some magical wealthy folks or entrepreneurs, make a commitment to spend more time with them. Ask them out for coffee, take them to lunch or dinner, or even book a consultation or coaching session with them to ask them how they got to where they are today. It's really inspiring to speak with people who have hacked the system and played the game by their own rules. So if you know someone successful, don't be shy. Sometimes people really enjoy sharing their wealth secrets with others.

If you don't know anyone who has become highly successful on their own terms, then there are other ways to learn from and be influenced by these people. Plenty of documentaries, self-help books, biographies, podcasts, and magazines talk about rags-to-riches stories, investing, business building, and wealth making. Seek out these kinds of resources. You can learn a lot from them and receive tons of powerful inspiration.

Instead of consuming social media or watching television, fill some of that time educating yourself about money management, entrepreneurship, sales/marketing, and different methods for creating sustainable wealth. This will help you keep your inner wealth garden watered and fertilized, and will keep you educated and inspired along the way.

———————— ❧ ————————

Finally, I want you to know it's never too late to re-create how you think and move in life and repattern your beliefs, especially when your progress is fueled by the power of angels. Every new day opens up the potential for incredible blessings and opportunities to expand in your life.

Remember, commit to your vision, believe in yourself, be audacious, be tenacious, and do what you can to continue to create the right environment for your inner wealth garden to flourish — so that the outside world can reflect the bounty and abundance that you have unlocked within you.

Now, are you ready to claim your next level of wealth and embark on your 11-Day Wealth Ritual? Say it with me: "I choose to be wealthy. I am wealthy." Take a moment and let yourself feel these words in your body as if you are indeed already wealthy. Let yourself feel wealthy, and know that the universe is conspiring to bring you wealth in magical ways.

Part II

YOUR 11-DAY WEALTH RITUAL

Kick Start

Angelic Banishing Ritual

Remember what mega-obstructionists your inner de-mons can be when it comes to your wealth magic? Well, it's time to officially expel these bad boys and kick off this 11-Day Wealth Ritual with a banishing ritual. You can think of a banishing ritual as a way to clear a bunch of weeds from your wealth garden all at once.

In traditional ceremonial magic, magicians have used banishing rituals to purify their spaces, their minds, and their intentions by eliminating negative mental and emotional influences like inner demons, fearful thoughts, worries, and doubts. However, the scope of a banishing ritual doesn't end there. Banishing rituals are also used for protection and the removal of dark spirits and energies from the home or from a person's psychic space.

The banishing ritual you are about to learn is a

simplified version of traditional banishing rituals, and it gets the job done. You can do it just once to kick off the eleven-day ritual, or you can use it daily if you enjoy it. It's really up to you. You should also know that magicians use banishing rituals when they just feel a little funky and want to clear the air so that they can feel better and more protected.

How to Get the Most Out of the Banishing Ritual

Before you complete this ritual, I want to remind you to keep an open heart and mind and approach it with child-like curiosity. Notice how you feel in your body and pay attention to the condition of your thoughts and feelings before performing this ritual. This will help you tune in to any positive changes that happen for you after the ritual is complete. Slowing down long enough to notice the positive shifts, even small shifts, is really half the battle when building a powerful relationship with angels, and I don't want you to miss the profound ways in which the angels can work for you. So please do pay attention to any signs that make you feel clearer, lighter, brighter, more hopeful, or safer.

Read through the whole ritual before you actually do it so you can get acquainted with the flow of the process first. When you are ready to officially perform the ritual, make sure you are in a place where you won't be interrupted. You can choose to do it in a room in your home or even in the great outdoors. If you want to enhance the mood for the banishing ritual, you can light a candle or even burn a little incense. It's your ritual, after all, so create the set and setting that feels the most luscious and inspiring for you.

For this banishing ritual, you will be working with six of the archangels: Raphael, Michael, Gabriel, Uriel, Metatron, and Sandalphon. These archangels can create a powerful field of divine protection around you...and, well, who doesn't want that? After all, we want all hands on deck to help you open the portal so you can rock your next level of wealth.

As you walk through the ritual, pay attention to which archangels seem to be more alive or present for you. Many people experience at least one or two archangels that come in stronger than the others. If you sense one more strongly, you may want to stay in contact with them throughout your wealth magic ritual process. They may have special support just for you, and there's nothing wrong with making new archangel friends along the way.

Now that I've laid some groundwork, it's time to get started with this awesomeness. Your ritual can take as long as you want. If you get really good at it, you will only need a few minutes, but for now, take it slow. Enjoy the process, and remember to come at it from a place of love, honoring, and curiosity.

Steps of the Angelic Banishing Ritual

1. Beginning the Ritual

First, you will need to orient yourself. We will be working with the cardinal directions, so take a moment to figure out where east, south, west, and north are in relation to where you are standing. If you have a smartphone, it most likely has a compass app that can help you find them.

Next, imagine yourself standing at the center of a large circle divided by an equilateral cross into four quadrants. Each line of the cross will point to one of the four cardinal directions. In just a moment, you will call in or invoke one of the archangels to stand at each quarter of the circle or in each cardinal direction, as well as above and below you.

Stand with your body open and receptive. Place your palms up, with your arms outstretched to the east, as if you are ready to receive something beautiful.

Next, imagine that you have long, strong roots coming out of your feet anchoring you down to the planet, and that with every breath, you naturally pull up cleansing and healing earth energy into your body.

Above you, imagine, sense, or visualize beautiful starlight cascading down into your head, through your body. Imagine this starlight getting mixed with the earth energy beneath you and within your body.

Before you invoke the archangels, I want you to close your eyes, let the room and the material world fall away, and imagine it's just you standing in the center of the universe. Feel the expansiveness, and bring yourself all the way into the present moment. Remember your powerful intention for wealth; allow yourself to feel the emotion of your big *whys*. Recall how important your *whys* are to you, and let yourself feel how wonderful it is to have the support of the angels. Enter your banishing ritual with an already grateful heart.

2. Calling In Archangel Raphael to the East

Now, it's time to call in our first archangel, Raphael.

Ask him to stand to the east so that he can give you fierce protection and healing during your wealth magic journey.

Stand facing the east. Call on Raphael by saying the archangel's name three times:

Archangel Raphael, Raphael, Raphael, please come and stand and protect me in the east.

Saying the name of the angel you are calling on three times helps you align with the energy of the angel and their frequency.

Imagine, feel, sense, hear, or visualize Archangel Raphael standing in the east. Raphael is known as the great healer among the archangels, and he is often associated with emerald-green light. Sometimes he is represented as carrying a caduceus (the snake-entwined staff that symbolizes medicine). If you want, you can work with this imagery as you call him in.

Once you get a sense that Raphael is with you, you can thank the archangel for his love and protection, speak your intention for wealth, and say anything else you'd like to say to him. When you feel or sense that your message has been received, thank Archangel Raphael for his help and ask him to keep supporting you.

When your work is complete in the east, it's time to move to your next direction, the south.

3. Calling In Archangel Michael to the South

Face the south with palms up; this is where Archangel Michael traditionally stands. You can call him by saying his name three times:

> *Archangel Michael, Michael, Michael, please stand with me and protect me in the south.*

Archangel Michael is traditionally depicted as the warrior of heaven who puts the smack down on evil. This includes dark thoughts, doubts, worries, and fears. Allow yourself to imagine him coming with full warrior gear, ready to do battle for you.

Feel, sense, and know that he has come to your side. Once you get a sense of this, thank Archangel Michael for joining you and share with him your wealth intention. Know that this archangel has your back for the duration of your wealth ritual. Once you feel that your work is done here, you are ready to do your work in the west.

4. Calling In Archangel Gabriel to the West

Archangel Gabriel traditionally stands in the west. Call on Gabriel by saying the archangel's name three times:

> *Archangel Gabriel, Gabriel, Gabriel, please come and stand and protect me in the west.*

Archangel Gabriel, whose name means "God is my strength," is known for many things. What's most notable about this archangel for our wealth purposes is that in your time of need Gabriel can help give you the courage and strength to take inspired action, which is radically important when it comes to pursuing your dreams.

Imagine, feel, sense, visualize, or just know that Gabriel stands with you in the west. The color blue is often associated with Gabriel, so feel free to work with that color in this quadrant. Once you get a sense that the archangel is standing guard in the west, thank Gabriel for coming, and share your wealth intention. Once you feel like your work is done here, it's time to face north.

5. Calling In Archangel Uriel to the North

Archangel Uriel traditionally stands in the north. Call him in with your intention and by saying the archangel's name three times:

Archangel Uriel, Uriel, Uriel, please come to my side; stand and protect me in the north.

Archangel Uriel, whose name means "the light of God," can bring you mental strength, clarity, and wisdom, and can inspire powerful new ideas. As you call him in, you can imagine him in bedazzling golden robes carrying a brilliant lamp radiating bright golden light.

When you get a sense that Uriel is with you, thank the archangel for coming and share your wealth intention. Once you feel like this exchange has concluded, it's time to move on to your next direction.

6. Calling In Archangel Metatron above You

Now that you have the four cardinal directions in order and you have created a circle of angelic protection for yourself, you can place your attention on the space above you, where Metatron shields you.

Archangel Metatron is an ultra badass, thought to assist in and support the flow of divine energy directly from Source down to the earth plane. Because of this, he is placed above you.

Face your palms upward as you call in this divine director, and say his name three times:

Archangel Metatron, Metatron, Metatron, please come to me and protect me from above.

You can imagine that a bright, crystalline light above you begins to grow. This is the light of the Creator/God/Source. Metatron brings this light through, making sure that your circle is protected by the energy of the Most High.

When you get a sense that the archangel is with you, thank him for coming, share your intention with him, and ask for his blessing.

Once you feel like this part is done, you are now ready to bring your awareness to the earth beneath you.

7. Calling In Archangel Sandalphon to the Earth

Archangel Sandalphon is known for watching over the earth realm, gathering the prayers of humans, and carrying them to the divine Creator. Because of this, Sandalphon is often thought to help with your manifesting power, which is quite important for your newfound commitment to attracting more wealth and success.

With this in mind, face your palms downward toward the earth. You can even bend over to touch the ground if you like. Call the name of Sandalphon three times:

Archangel Sandalphon, Sandalphon, Sandalphon, please come to me and protect me from below.

Feel, sense, or visualize a powerful angelic presence beneath you. You can also imagine that this angel wears the beautiful colors of the earth, browns or russets or forest greens, if this visual helps you.

When you get a sense that Sandalphon is with you, thank him for coming and center your awareness into your heart.

8. Completing the Ritual

Now that you have called in the archangels and their protection from all six directions, allow yourself to feel the sense of security all around you, as if you are wrapped in a big, beautiful bubble of healing and protection. Remember your intention for wealth and let yourself feel as if the wealth that you are asking for has already materialized. Let your whole body feel this intention as if it has already manifested. Then give one final thank-you to the archangels.

Next, I want you to check in with yourself. Did you notice any positive shifts after your banishing ritual? Did one or two of the archangels come through for you any stronger than the others? If so, remember to document all your results in your magical grimoire.

Now that you have magically banished negativity, are you ready to kick off day 1 of the wealth ritual? Good. Let's do this!

Guidelines for Your
11-Day Wealth Ritual

Now that you've cleared the air with the Angelic Banishing Ritual, the time has finally arrived for you to set this 11-Day Wealth Ritual in motion. Ready to grow some cabbage?

Over the last few chapters, you have planted the seeds for your wealth garden to grow. And you have met the dazzling wealth angels who will help you make big shifts on the inside so that you can more easily manifest wealth on the outside. Over the next eleven days, you will continue your work with the angels of wealth. You'll be working with many of the angels you met in chapter 3, as well as a surprise guest.

Each day of this eleven-day ritual includes an invocation and an angel meditation/activation. You will need only ten to fifteen minutes a day to complete these rituals. You can read through my meditation prompts, or if you prefer a guided meditation, you can go to my Angel Wealth Magic resources page to download the audio recording of each one: AngelWealthMagic.com/Resources.

You also will need blank copies of your magic mirror for a couple of these days. You can print them out from the website link, or you can draw the concentric circles yourself.

Once you begin day 1 of the ritual, it's important that you complete this ritual from start to finish, all the way to day 11. Each day was channeled by me in this specific order, and each day builds upon the last. So please do the days in order — don't skip around. If you accidentally miss a day or two for some reason, you can either pick up where you left off or start from the beginning, whichever feels best for you, as long as you eventually get to day 11 and complete the ritual.

If you generally struggle with consistency, here are some tips to help you. Choose a specific time of day that you want to perform the ritual, and set a daily alarm for that time on your watch or phone. You may also want to book out the time officially in your calendar to help give you extra incentive. Remember, *commitment* is one of the main ingredients necessary for this kind of magic to work for you. Consider this eleven-day ritual your first test in showing yourself and your invisible allies your commitment to growing in wealth.

Have fun with the process, and keep your eyes and ears open for signs that your wealth magic is working! Say it with me: "I am wealthy!"

Close your eyes, and feel the truth of this statement in your body.

Now, if you're ready, let's get to it — day 1.

Day 1

Archangel Raziel

Open the Portal

Welcome to day 1 of your 11-Day Wealth Ritual! To get this wealth party started right, we are going to kick off this ritual with Archangel Raziel. Considered the grand magician of the archangels, he is the master of esoteric wisdom and the laws of the universe.

We are starting with Raziel because he's known to act as a bridge between humans and the angelic realm. By calling on him first, you are, in a sense, asking him to open the floodgates of communication between you and the angelic world. We want to make sure that your requests are being heard loud and clear by your angels and wealth allies, which is what this amazing archangel is all about.

Before we do this activation with Archangel Raziel, I want you to remember why you are here. Remember the amount of cashola you're working to magically manifest and allow yourself to feel the emotion you hold toward it and your desire for it.

We're now ready to open up the portal for this eleven-day ritual to officially begin. OK, then, let's get ready to meet Archangel Raziel.

Find a quiet spot to do this work, and when you're ready, say this invocation out loud.

Day 1 Invocation

Creator of All That Is, the angels and allies of wealth, and especially you, dear Archangel Raziel, I ask you to open the portal of direct communication between me and the angelic realm. I ask that this channel be held in the energy and with the protection and strength of the Creator. I ask that my intention of _____ [state your intention] be heard and fulfilled with swiftness and grace, and that any materialization of wealth lead me closer to love and to my mission. This is the beginning. I now open the way. Thank you, Raziel.

Next, either you can listen to the free guided meditation audio that I have provided to you for day 1 or you can perform the following meditation on your own.

Audio meditation available at
AngelWealthMagic.com/Resources

Day 1 Meditation

Close your eyes, center yourself, sit quietly, and say Raziel's name three times to align you with his energy.

Next, imagine a beautiful landscape with a giant tree that stretches so high in the sky that it may even touch the stars. This tree has a strong, wide trunk, and you get the sense that it's powerfully rooted into the ground.

Now, take your awareness to the very top of this great tree. You can feel, see, or simply get a sense of it. As you do, imagine clouds beginning to roll in above the tree, almost like an electrical storm is growing in power, converging on this great tree. Allow yourself to get a sense that Archangel Raziel is in the center of this storm, summoning power from all corners of the universe and all four quarters. As he collects this power, a bright blue electrical storm begins crackling in the clouds. You have a sense that the electricity is powerful, but not harmful to you.

Next, you can welcome Raziel and ask him to open the doorway of communication between you and the angels. You can make this request out loud or silently, whichever feels better for you. After you do so, imagine that a beautiful electric-blue bolt of lightning comes down through the top of your head and into the center of your chest. When you feel the lightning there, imagine that a six-pointed star inside your heart lights up with the blue flame. If you know what a Star of David looks like, feel free to work with that image if it helps.

Allow this blue flame to burn brightly inside your

heart and then allow the brightness to grow to envelop your body. Allow yourself to feel a deeper sense of love and protection as you walk your path toward growing in wealth.

In your mind, hold your intention for the amount of money you'd like to attract, imagining that all that money has already come to you. Imagine that amount sitting in your bank account right now.

Next, ask Raziel to open the lines of communication with the angels over the course of these eleven days and ensure that each angel and ally you call upon hears your prayers and shows up strongly for you.

When you are done, thank Raziel for coming to you and helping you and let him know he may go in peace. Gently bring yourself back into the room…and *voilà*: your first day is complete!

Take out your grimoire and write down "Day 1." Write the amount of cash you are welcoming in and circle it. Next, note any relevant thoughts, feelings, ideas, or sensations that arose for you during this activation.

Now that you are done with day 1, keep your eyes and ears open for signs that your wealth magic is working.

May you receive all the wealth you are asking for and more.

See you tomorrow on day 2.

Day 2

Nitika

Bring On the Cash

Welcome to day 2 of this miraculous wealth ritual! Today I get to introduce you to one of my secret wealth weapons, Nitika. This spirit is among my faves by far, because they were one of the key wealth allies that helped me manifest that miraculous $150K I mentioned earlier in the book.

In traditional old-school magic, Nitika is not an angel but is said to be an embodiment of the Virtues. My experience of Nitika is they are gentle and loving yet extremely powerful. Nitika can help you unlock funds that are out there but you may have forgotten about, or didn't even know existed, and can also inspire you to take a variety of actions that can help you attract some cold, hard cashola. This magical money manifestation can happen pretty quickly from this spirit, so keep your eyes peeled.

Nitika works best when you have a specific sum in

mind, so be sure to settle on an intended dollar amount ahead of time. You will also need to be in touch with how you would like to spend your cash once you have it. This helps make it feel more real. You will be sharing these details with Nitika once you invoke them.

Before we call in Nitika, have one of the blank magic mirrors handy (see page 42 for more on this). Write the name "Nitika" on it in the center. If for some reason you can't print or make a copy of the magic mirror now, no worries. A quick drawing of the sigil circles will work just fine.

Ready to call in Nitika? Say this invocation out loud.

Day 2 Invocation

In the name of the Creator of All That Is, I call on the spirit of Nitika to come to my side. Dearest Nitika, I welcome you into my life and ask that you bring me $_____ [specific amount]. I ask that you shape time and space, the present and the future, to make this happen. I plan to use this money by _____ [date]. I thank you deeply, in the name of God/universe/Creator.

Next, either you can listen to the free guided meditation audio that I have provided to you for day 2 or you can perform the following meditation on your own.

Audio meditation available at
AngelWealthMagic.com/Resources

Day 2 Magic Mirror Meditation

Have your magic mirror handy.

Close your eyes, center yourself, sit quietly, and say Nitika's name three times to align yourself with their energy.

Look at the magic mirror and imagine that the inner circle is a window and that Nitika is standing on the other side of that window.

While focusing on the white space in the center of the inner circle (not on the letters of the name), imagine that you are connecting with Source and with Nitika, as if you are looking into a portal to the Divine. Imagine Nitika has heard you. Say hello to Nitika and thank them for coming and for listening.

Share your intention for the specific cash amount you are calling in. Allow yourself to feel a sense of urgency concerning this money. Use your emotion.

Next, focus on the white space in the outer rim of the circle. As you do, consciously make the choice to manifest your intention with magic. Embody the feeling of making this choice and the sense of resolve you feel when you do.

Look at the name in the center of the circle. Look at the letters of the name N-I-T-I-K-A and embody the sense that your intention has already manifested.

Now, open your gaze to the whole magic mirror. Let your vision blur a bit and take in the entire thing. Imagine that ten years from now, all your money issues are 100 percent resolved. Imagine that you have more cash than you really need and that your biggest problem is trying to figure out what to do with it. Feel the feeling of having way more than you need and the safety and relaxation that comes with it. Feel the feeling of having let money struggles go years ago, confident that those problems are a thing of the past.

After you're done, thank Nitika for listening to your intention and for helping you. You can then ask them to go in peace. Feel, sense, and know that Nitika has left and is getting to work for you.

If this first round of the process felt a little clunky, feel free to do it again. After you are done with this process, write "Day 2" in your grimoire, write the amount of cash you are manifesting, and circle it. Then sit quietly and jot down any thoughts and feelings that came up for you.

✤

Now that you are done with day 2, keep your eyes and ears open for signs that your wealth magic is working.

May you receive all the cashola you are asking for and more.

See you tomorrow on day 3.

Day 3

Archangel Jophiel

Massive Optimism

Today, we are going to work with Jophiel, the angel of beauty, who can help you achieve a massively optimistic outlook no matter what is happening in life. Remember Jophiel from chapter 3? Yeah, well, Jophiel is the bomb-dot-com. Other magicians and I have worked with her for years to help open the pathway to a positive mindset.

As a matter of fact, whenever I ask wealthy people to share their secrets of success, they never start with action steps, strategy, or anything like that. They usually begin talking about mindset first. That's because, like we discussed earlier in the book, wealth truly does begin on the inside, with a magical mindset.

Your ability to stay optimistic and *believe* in yourself and your vision is so incredibly important in achieving your next level of wealth that the angels inspired me to dedicate a whole day just to help you learn this essential. Remember, believing amazing things are possible for you, even in the face of adversity, *is* a choice you can make.

Today, Archangel Jophiel wants to give you a big boost of beautiful optimism to help you feel more hopeful about yourself, your worth, your abilities, your gift to the world, and even life itself. Jophiel wants to help you shift the deepest part of your heart and mind back to the positive pole. She can help you find the beauty in at least trying to move in the direction of happiness, fulfillment, and a deep sense of purpose.

So say goodbye to the ol' doom and gloom, and open your heart and mind to the beauty and the positivity that is Archangel Jophiel. Are you ready for the invocation? Say it out loud.

———————— ❧ ————————

Day 3 Invocation

Dear Creator and Archangel Jophiel, I ask you to enter the deepest parts of my heart and mind, my life, and my bank account, and attune all these things with the energy and power of true optimism. Help me see the beauty of my life and my potential. Help me see the beauty of who I am, and help me experience the joy and fun of taking big, beautiful, positive risks. I am ready to experience myself and my life in new and beautiful ways. I thank you for coming to me today, dear Jophiel.

❧

Next, either you can listen to the free guided meditation audio that I have provided to you for day 3 or you can perform the following meditation on your own.

Audio meditation available at
AngelWealthMagic.com/Resources

---- ✤ ----

Day 3 Meditation

Close your eyes, center yourself, sit quietly, and say Jophiel's name three times to help bring in her amazing vibe.

Feel, sense, see, or just know that Archangel Jophiel has entered the space with you. Take your time to feel or perceive the color of light that she brings with her today. What color do you sense now? If you can't see it, it's OK. You don't have to. Sometimes you get something as simple as a hunch or a quick thought of a color. Sense it and trust that you are perceiving things correctly.

Now I want you to feel or sense a set of invisible eyeglasses sitting over your eyes. Perceive these glasses as if they are your old way of seeing yourself, your life, and your potential. Get a sense that these glasses feel uncomfortable or too tight or are way too outdated.

Now take a deep breath, and with the exhale allow Jophiel to remove those tired old glasses. Continue to breathe until you feel, sense, or know that something has shifted.

She then replaces your glasses with a very cool set

with colored lenses. Archangel Jophiel tells you that this is your special color and vibration to achieve massive optimism.

Take a moment for your eyes to fully drink in this color and receive this vibration as an electrical current into your brain and down through your nervous system. Allow it to flow through your organs, your bones…through all the cells of your body, all the way down to the tips of your toes.

Bask in the glory of having a beautiful heart and mind filled with optimism.

Gently open your eyes and take in the beauty of the space around you, even if it's a messy house. *Choose* to see beauty and optimism with the help of Jophiel — the power to *choose*, as you know, is everything.

Thank Archangel Jophiel and ask her to help keep your new, beautiful, and optimistic attitude alive and well in all your endeavors.

⚜

After your meditation, write down "Day 3" in your grimoire, write the amount of cash you are manifesting, and circle it. Then sit quietly and jot down any thoughts and feelings that came up for you through your work with Jophiel.

Now that you are done with day 3, keep your eyes and ears open for signs that your wealth magic is working.

May you receive all the wealth you are asking for and more. Let the greenbacks flow!

See you tomorrow on day 4.

Day 4

Rahnahdiel

Release Guilt, Shame, and Unworthiness

Today we dive deep into helping you disarm some of the sneaky inner demons that we mentioned earlier in the book — those demons that could be blocking you from receiving your full harvest of wealth awesomeness.

As we have discussed, thoughts and feelings of unworthiness, shame, and even guilt could be lurking underneath your desire for more cash. It's emotions just like these that can energetically block you from making the audacious power moves to amass more wealth. And let's be honest: if you aren't making power moves in your life, you definitely aren't going to be shattering your wealth ceiling.

In order to address this, today I'm introducing you to not just any angel but an angel who is said to embody the power of *several* angels. Rahnahdiel can help you receive more cash by helping you release deep-seated guilt, shame, and unworthiness that may be blocking you from your wealth goals.

I recently came across a quote by an anonymous poster that reminded me of what the powers of Rahnahdiel can help you with: "The death of misconception allows the birth of authentic power." Ending your misconceptions about yourself and your life may seem challenging at first, but not when you get to work with powerful angels like Rahnahdiel.

Now it's time to dispel your misconceptions with this angelic heavy and open the road to receiving even more of your massive and shameless bounty.

Ready for the invocation? Say it out loud when you are.

Day 4 Invocation

Dear Creator of All That Is, Rahnahdiel, and all the angels and allies of wealth, abundance, and harvest, I ask you to release me from the imprisonment of guilt, shame, and unworthiness. Help clear my vessel in the name of the Most High so that I may embody a true state of receptivity toward my next level of wealth. I'm so grateful for your healing and blessing today.

Next, either you can listen to the free guided meditation audio that I have provided to you for day 4 or you can perform the following meditation on your own.

--- ✤ ---

Day 4 Meditation

Say Rahnahdiel's name three times. This helps focus your energy and opens the lines of communication.

Relax, center yourself, and sink into the sensations of your body. Allow your body to show you where a dark web of guilt, shame, and feelings of unworthiness live inside you. Perceive this dark web through your inner vision or feelings and observe it without judgment. You may notice a sense of heaviness, a tightness, or perhaps a temperature change in your body. This is OK. Your task here is to simply observe how these feelings want to manifest for you today, without judgment.

Next, call in Rahnahdiel to help release you from this web of emotions. Wait until you feel, sense, or know that they are with you.

Now speak to the angel from the heart. Let this angel know of your struggle with these darker emotions and that you are tired of limiting yourself and feeling bad. Let them know that you are ready to let these feelings go, that they no longer serve you. Ask Rahnahdiel to help you shift them into personal power and make you a more receptive vessel for wealth. You can say anything else that you feel compelled to say to this angel.

Next, sense Rahnahdiel releasing you from this bondage by filling your body with a bright golden light. Make sure to breathe through your belly and witness, allow, sense, or feel this work being done.

Next, imagine that this web begins changing from a dark color into luminous gold, almost as if golden rivers of confidence, wealth, and worthiness flow. Take your time with this part until you sense that there has been a shift.

When the work feels complete, thank Rahnahdiel for coming, and ask them to keep working with you to attune you even more to being a wealth magnet. Let them know they can go in peace.

Slowly come back into your body and notice how you feel.

⚜

Do you feel lighter? Make sure to whip out your grimoire, write "Day 4" in it, write the amount of cash you are manifesting, and circle it. Then sit quietly and jot down any thoughts and feelings that came up for you.

Boom! Now that you are done with day 4, keep your eyes and ears open for signs that your wealth magic is working.

May you receive all the wealth you are asking for and more.

See you tomorrow on day 5.

Day 5

Sitael and Poiel

Reverse Misfortune, Cancel Curses,
and Become a Money Magnet

Welcome to day 5! You are almost halfway through! Can you believe it? So many folks have a hard time sticking to their word and honoring their commitment to acquire more wealth, but not you. The angels of wealth and I applaud you for your determination to make it all the way to day 5.

So let's talk about the fortune of your fortunes. If you feel cursed in the finance department, don't worry; lots of folks do. But today we have an angelic power duo coming in to help you reverse any history of misfortune and financial trauma. But that's just the beginning — we'll also be boosting your capacity to have even more wealth and success.

Today you work with Sitael and Poiel. Sitael is stepping up to the plate to help you cancel any strings of bad financial luck you have had in your life. If you feel like your business, vision, or bank account is cursed or stuck, then this angel is a huge ally.

Sitael also wants me to bring your attention to how in the past, you may have been sabotaging your wealth potential with negative thoughts about yourself, your cash flow, your business, or your dreams. If you discovered earlier in the book that your love for money could use improvement, today will definitely be helpful to you.

As Sitael helps you let go of misfortune, we welcome the angel Poiel, who wants to bring you good financial luck. Poiel can help you open the gates of abundance and attract fortune of all kinds to you. They can also help you materialize your heart's deepest desires and feel hopeful about your financial future.

In addition, this angel is known to help convert your talents and gifts into fame, fortune, and celebrity. So if you are an artist, writer, speaker, teacher, healer, or anything else along these lines, Poiel can help you become highly esteemed in your field and reach celebrity status with work that makes your soul sing. Not only that, but if you have an extra-fun hobby that you have been daydreaming about, this angel can help you monetize it.

All this sound tasty? Great! Go ahead and say the invocation out loud.

Day 5 Invocation

Creator of All That Is and Sitael, I ask you to enter my heart, mind, and life and to cancel, clear, remove, and neutralize any misfortune or financial curses from my past, present, and future. I ask you to ensure that I permanently leave any bad luck or misfortune behind me.

Creator of All That Is and Poiel, I ask that you lead me down the road to massive fortune and good luck. Help elevate my gifts and talents, my communication, and my individual genius to align with the highest and best version of my life and my work. I'm grateful for your help and am ready to receive all the good that's coming to me and more. Thank you.

✤

Next, you can listen to the free guided meditation audio that I have provided to you for day 5 or you can perform the following meditation on your own.

Audio meditation available at
AngelWealthMagic.com/Resources

──────── ✤ ────────

Day 5 Meditation

First, I want you to feel into any negative thoughts you have about money or any bad luck or misfortune you have experienced.

Close your eyes, center yourself, sit quietly, and say Sitael's name three times. Imagine this angel standing with you. Share your struggles, any misfortunes, and even your regrets about money or past choices you have made.

Ask Sitael to release you from these memories, thoughts, and feelings once and for all so that you can be free. Take your time with this.

Imagine, sense, or see Sitael by your side. Imagine that they wave a lamp with bright golden light around your head. As the light penetrates your skin, notice a kind of sludge or slime draining down from you. Allow this lamplight to move slowly through your body: down your neck, shoulders, chest, back, arms, belly, legs...eventually all the way down to your toes. Allow the sludge to leave your feet and be drained deep into the soil of the earth. Make sure to breathe through this, and with every exhale, let a little more go. With every breath, get a sense that that old energy is leaving you.

Next, call in Poiel by saying their name three times. Imagine them standing there with you holding a large magician's wand. Share your deepest desires for success and wealth with Poiel. This may feel weird to you in the beginning, but imagine that this angel is 100 percent nonjudgmental and unconditionally loving. Let yourself share your most grandiose dreams and desires. Don't hold back. Take your time. And please do remember to ask for massive good fortune — I mean, why not?

When Poiel has heard your wishes and intentions, they will point their wand to your heart, illuminating it and opening you up more fully to your own innate power and essential nature. They remind you that the key to wealth is always inside you. Notice what color light you see or sense. That color represents your vision of wealth. Breathe deeply as Poiel attunes your heart to the energy of good fortune and to your own divine talents, gifts, and genius. Allow this light to swell within your chest until you feel, sense, know, or see that the work is complete.

Thank Poiel and Sitael for coming, and ask them to keep doing this work for you. Let them know they can go in peace, and slowly come back into your full consciousness.

❧

Now, on a scale of 1 to 10, how negative do you feel about your wealth? Any improvement? If not, keep chipping away at it.

Write "Day 5" in your grimoire, write the amount of cash you are manifesting, and circle it. Then sit quietly and jot down any thoughts, feelings, sensations, or inspirations that came up for you.

Wonderful! Now that you are done with day 5, keep your eyes and ears open for signs that your wealth magic is working.

May you receive all the wealth you are asking for and more.

See you tomorrow on day 6.

Day 6

Veuliah

The Right Kind of Wealth

Today's invocation will help you attract not just wealth but the *right kind* of wealth. And what I mean by that is wealth that enriches and supports your happiness, as well as wealth that is conscientious and ethical.

We have all seen some wealthy folks acting the fool out there, getting all greedy and weird. As a matter of fact, as you've no doubt noticed, sometimes wealth, fame, and success can lead to isolation, depression, and extreme abuses of power. All of that is quite simply not the wealth vibe we are looking for. We want you to have wealth that uplifts your life and nourishes you and the folks around you.

Today the angels and I want to address this by introducing an angel that can attune you to the right kind of wealth — the kind that is yummy and juicy, and also linked to a service or offering you can gift to the world.

Spirit shows me that for any individual, there is more than one road to wealth. There are actually *many* opportunities and options for you to uplevel your wealth capacity. The angel Veuliah, however, can attune you to your highest and best path toward wealth — one that keeps your heart open and brings you, your family, and the people you serve more love and support. Think of wealth that comes from incredible altruism and integrity so that you can walk a noble path and be more loving, open, and generous along the way. Sound good?

Now, on a cool side note, this angel isn't simply about love and altruism. Veuliah can also be a fierce warrior and protector. They will furiously defend those they serve — as in *you*. Modern and ancient magicians alike have historically worked with this angel to stop bullies and repel enemies. I wanted to mention this because big expansion in your life can often trigger the folks around you. When you make power moves and become more visible, you might notice a few extra haters or trolls in your midst. It simply comes with the territory when you become more successful. Veuliah can help you block the negativity so that you can focus on the good stuff and weave your special brand of magic in the world. I just love me some angels!

Before we start, print one of your blank magic mirrors or draw the sigil, write the name "Veuliah" in the middle of the circles, and have it ready for when we are doing today's activation.

Say the invocation below out loud and get ready to soak in this angel's goodness.

Day 6 Invocation

Dear Creator of All That Is, the angels and allies of wealth, and angel Veuliah, I ask you to come to my side so that you can align my intentions for wealth with my highest ideals. Help me be joyous and noble as I walk the path toward more wealth. Help me be of highest and best service to my family, my friends, my community, and the world. I also ask that you give me fierce protection along my wealth journey. Help me feel safe and help me open up to extraordinary, miraculous, and massive wealth. I thank you for listening to my plea.

✤

Next, either you can listen to the free guided meditation audio that I have provided to you for day 6 or you can perform the following meditation on your own.

Audio meditation available at
AngelWealthMagic.com/Resources

Day 6 Magic Mirror Meditation

Grab your magic mirror with the name of the angel on it.

Concentrate on the white space in the center of the circle. Choose one point if you can, and imagine that the white space is a window or portal to the angelic world.

Close your eyes, center yourself, and say the name Veuliah three times.

As you do this, imagine that this angel is on the other side of this magic mirror. Feel or sense that this amazing being is waiting for instructions.

As you focus, remember the intention and the amount of cash that you are manifesting. Telepathically show this angel how much cash you are attracting. Then request that this money and all the wealth that comes into your life be filled with love, integrity, and the noblest of intentions. Ask this angel to support you in your service to your family, your community, and the world. And ask that this wealth bring amazing love, support, and joy into your life and the lives of those around you. You will also want to ask for protection as you walk this wealth journey. If there is someone in your life who is particularly negative, now is a good time to ask for help with this specific person.

Move your gaze to the outer rim of the magic mirror, hold your gaze there, and commit to manifesting this cash amount with magic. Let your body really feel your resolve about this choice.

Next, go back to the center of the circle and focus just on the letters of the angel's name. As you do, imagine that your intention has already manifested. Imagine that the cash amount is in your hands and makes you feel happy, loved, and supported.

Allow yourself to feel an expansion of love and extraordinary gratitude. Let yourself feel the feeling that somehow this wealth inspires you to be of even more service to your family, your community, and the world.

For the last step, hold your wealth intention in your

mind, take a big breath, and "blow" your vision and intention ten years into your future. Imagine that it is a decade from now and you are well past the wealth level that you are asking for today. Let your body actually experience what it feels like to have more money than you need. Look back at yourself today as if it were the old days, and feel reverence for how far you have come.

After you feel like this work is complete, you can thank the angel Veuliah, ask them to go in peace, and ask them to keep supporting you along your journey. Wait until you get a sense that Veuliah heard your plea and has left to get to work for you.

❧

Grab your grimoire, write "Day 6" on it, write the amount of cash you are manifesting, and circle it. Then sit quietly and jot down any thoughts and feelings that came up for you.

All right! Now that you are done with day 6, keep your eyes and ears open for signs that your wealth magic is working.

May you receive all the wealth you are asking for and more.

See you tomorrow on day 7.

Day 7

Harachel

*Intellectual Abundance and Access
to Knowledge*

L et's face it, after decades of working hard and trying to juggle all your responsibilities, it's just so easy to lose your creativity. The grind at work and at home can zap your inspiration and rob you of your connection to that creative space inside you — that creative space that has all the solutions you'll ever need and more. Have you ever heard the maxim "Everything you need is already inside you" or "What you seek is within you"? Well, today's ritual is all about connecting you with the intelligence and creative genius that dwell inside you.

Many self-made wealthy folks have honed the ability to harness the power of their out-of-the-box creative ideas. They begin envisioning life outside the day-to-day grind and the golden handcuffs, and at some point they stop waiting around for someone else to give them a 3 percent annual raise. They instead follow an inspired idea or ideas and, like a magician, use the power of their intellect to shape an entirely new reality for themselves. *This is true life artistry.*

And much like an artist is free to execute their art without limits, so are you. Your best magic always begins with your powerful imagination and intellect — which brings me to our next angelic wealth asset, Harachel. Harachel is known to flood the magician who calls on them with a fountain of inspired ideas. They can help you manifest cash money by increasing your smarts and expanding your vision, while leading you to discover creative strategies for making your wealth dreams come true.

This angel can also help you be successful in your heart-centered work and at the same time enhance your sphere of influence within your family and social or work circles. All juicy stuff when it comes to creating your next level of wealth.

So without further ado, let's get ready for the invocation; bring on Harachel!

Day 7 Invocation

Creator of All That Is, the angels and allies of wealth, and angel Harachel, I ask you to unlock my divine intelligence and help me to clearly identify my best and highest ideas that will lead me to profound joy, wealth, and service. Help me become a true life artist and craft a life that exceeds my wildest expectations and dreams. I thank you for hearing my plea.

❦

Next, either you can listen to the free guided meditation audio that I have provided to you for day 7 or you can perform the following meditation on your own.

Audio meditation available at
AngelWealthMagic.com/Resources

--- ⚜ ---

Day 7 Meditation

Close your eyes, center yourself, and imagine, feel, or sense a great chain wrapped around your head with a lock keeping it in place. Wait until you actually get a sense of this.

Say Harachel's name three times, and as they come close to you, imagine them unlocking this chain so that it falls away from you. Make sure to connect with your breath; take a few deep breaths as the chain falls away.

Next, notice that Harachel holds a great book in their hands that seems to be illuminated with golden light from within. You sense that this book contains all the good ideas that you will ever need to be joyful, to be in love with life, to be wealthy, and to be a true life artist. This is a book of divine inspiration, as well as the Creator's will for your life.

Imagine this angel touching this massive book to your brow. Give Harachel permission to fill you with the fountain of inspiration, wisdom, and genius found within this book so that your intellectual capacity and creativity can expand, allowing you to achieve your next level of wealth.

Accept this gift as if you are drinking in this divine intelligence and creativity. Let yourself feel, sense, or know that you are filling yourself with the energy of this divine brilliance.

Now take a moment and talk to Harachel about where in your life you need to become more creative, more inspired, and more intelligent. Show them all the areas of your life where you need this help.

Next, imagine a beautiful garden inside you that is now full of fragrant, freshly sprouted plants that represent amazing ideas. Feel that in the moment you have everything you need to make your biggest dreams come true — dreams that will generate all the wealth you need and more. Take your time until you really feel this on an intellectual level, an emotional level, and even a physical level.

Thank Harachel for hearing you and ask them to help you keep generating the divine intelligence that you need in order to amass extraordinary wealth. Let them know that they can go in peace, and wait until you feel, sense, or know that they are gone.

✤

Grab your grimoire, write "Day 7" on it, write the amount of cash you are manifesting, and circle it. Then sit quietly and jot down any thoughts and feelings that came up for you.

Excellent! Now that you are done with day 7, keep your eyes and ears open for signs that your wealth magic is working.

May you receive all the wealth you are asking for and more.

See you tomorrow on day 8.

Day 8

Vehuiah and Mumiah

Willpower and Leadership

Now that your angels are working on helping you with big, beautiful, wealthy ideas, it's time to take the next step and talk about a couple of key qualities that most wealthy folk seem to have: willpower and leadership.

Once a wealthy person receives an epic idea, what do they do with it? Well, it's pretty clear that they don't just sit around and pray for Jesus or the angels to come rescue them. As we talked about earlier in the book, they know that *they* are the only one who can lead the show. They prioritize their epic dream and their big idea, and they understand that in order to lead and inspire others, they must first be adept at leading themselves.

Honestly, most folks don't always exhibit a high level of willpower and can be flaky when it comes to investing in their own dreams. Family, children, relationships, and just working on our daily responsibilities can suck the motivation out of us. And, of course, the sneaky inner demons don't help the cause at all. It's no wonder that it can be so easy for folks to put their dreams on hold while the circus of life constantly cages them in the status quo.

Well, status quo *no más*!

Which leads me to our luscious angels of the day, Vehuiah and Mumiah. They are joining forces today to help take your willpower and your leadership to the next level. Together these angels can help you stay powerfully determined, enhance your personal discipline, and give you the strength, focus, and tenacity to make your dreams come true.

Vehuiah loves working with leaders and helping them know their power, lead from the heart, and become more successful in all their endeavors. It is said that repeating this angel's name can activate the energy of your true divine will and your life purpose, and can align you with your unique brand of leadership and success. They can also help any project that you are working on become more successful.

And just in case you need even more determination to take action on your delightful wealth ideas, the angel Mumiah is here for you. If you often find yourself feeling unmotivated, this angel can give you the courage, willpower, and especially the audacity to turn these dreams into reality. And get this: not only does Mumiah help with all the stuff I just mentioned, but they can also help protect you and your project from negative energy or influences that may want to lure you away from your commitment.

Ready to meet these two angelic heavies? Say the invocation below out loud.

Day 8 Invocation

Dear Creator, the angels and allies of wealth, Vehuiah, and Mumiah, I ask you to come close to me and help me execute my True Will. I ask to be attuned with my highest level of leadership and success. Give me the strength, courage, audacity, and focus to create my wealthiest and happiest life. Help me turn my big ideas into reality and release me from overwhelm, confusion, and anything else that stands in my way. And help me walk this path of love with willpower and determination so that I finish what I start with joy and ease. I thank you for coming to me today.

Next, either you can listen to the free guided meditation audio that I have provided to you for day 8 or you can perform the following meditation on your own.

Audio meditation available at
AngelWealthMagic.com/Resources

Day 8 Meditation

First, notice how your body feels. Do you feel depleted or tired, blocked or tense? Then notice the quality of your mind. Is it busy? Does it have a hard time settling down? Just notice without attachment or judgment. Take a moment to observe how you are doing in this moment.

Next, I want you to allow yourself to feel your desire for your next level of wealth. If you tend to flake out on yourself, you can even feel into that sense of disappointment. Remember, in magic your negative emotions are just as valuable as your positive emotions, so always bring your full self to this process without judgment. After you've allowed yourself to feel your emotions regarding your wealth intention, dream, or big idea, you are ready for the next step.

Begin calling in Vehuiah by saying the name out loud. Not just three times but over and over again like it's a mantra. You can even sing the name if this helps you stay more focused and feel more emotion. (Angels do love them some singing!)

As you repeat the name Vehuiah over and over again, I want you to imagine that the sound and the associated vibrations begin moving through your body from the top of your head down to the tips of your toes, permeating the cells of your organs, your bones, and all your body.

Invite Vehuiah and their beautiful qualities to come to life within you. Feel, sense, or know that this angel is alive within you.

Next, ask Vehuiah for a big boost of energy, confidence, and concentration with regard to your dreams and your wealth intention. Ask for the strength to execute your divine will and the Creator's plan for you. Ask Vehuiah to free you from any flakiness and, in exchange, to give you self-determination and self-leadership. Ask them to help you be a stronger leader for your own sake and that of anyone else who benefits from your leadership.

Now make the *choice* to become self-determined, to become a strong self-leader, and to once and for all let go of flaking on yourself. I want you to feel this decision being made in your body and wait until you perceive this change.

Next, it's time to reach out to Mumiah. Ask this angel to come to you. You're going to keep saying the name Mumiah until you feel, sense, or know that this presence is with you. Now invite this energy to come to life inside you and inside every cell of your body. We're going to ask Mumiah to help you finish those projects that are important to you. Ask them to release you from over-whelm and any distractions that are blocking you from fulfilling your heart's greatest desires.

Take a moment until you feel that your intentions have been understood, and allow yourself to feel, sense, or know that Mumiah has heard you.

Finally, thank both of these amazing angels for coming, and allow yourself to experience what this next level of leadership feels like for you. Know that you are bound for success with all these amazing angels and allies you are meeting along the way.

✤

Now grab your grimoire, write "Day 8" on it, write the amount of cash you are manifesting, and circle it. Then sit quietly and jot down any thoughts and feelings that came up for you.

Now that you are done with day 8, keep your eyes and ears open for signs that your wealth magic is working.

May you receive all the wealth you are asking for and more.

See you tomorrow on day 9.

Day 9

Yeyayel and Lauviah

Fame and Celebrity

Welcome back to your amazing wealth ritual! Now that you have what it takes to embody the qualities of a fiercely determined, divinely guided leader, today I'm introducing you to a power duo of fame, celebrity, fortune, and success.

Now, just hearing the words *fame* and *celebrity* may ignite a little resistance in you. As a matter of fact, achieving celebrity and fame may not even be in the top one hundred on your bucket list. However, a certain level of celebrity also means that you have some manner of influence, and influence is one of the traits that help the wealthy become wealthier.

Before I go further, I want to acknowledge that you don't have to be a celebrity or even be famous in order to amass wealth. However, the angels are extending an invitation for you to open up to this possibility. A *celebrity* is, quite simply, someone who is celebrated. Wouldn't you like to feel honored and celebrated by your family? By your peers? By your clients? By your colleagues? By your boss? By your angel investors or the venture capitalists who may want to fund your big idea?

The angels you are about to meet can enhance your overall reputation, both personally and professionally. This can open the door to wielding more influence within your circles, gaining access to more resources, and feeling more loved, respected, and appreciated for who you are and what you do.

Sound juicy? Good, let's meet them.

First, allow me to introduce Yeyayel. This angel brings success, fame, and celebrity all wrapped up in one. Yeyayel can boost your reputation, improve your sense of leadership, and if you are shy and introverted, help you become more confident so you have a commanding presence.

Next up is the angel Lauviah. Lauviah can help give you, your ideas, and your business a big boost of magnetism so that you can attract the right kind of opportunities and people. They can also help you attract more clients or a broader audience if you have a business that can benefit from this.

So let's get ready to invoke these angelic badasses.

———————— ✤ ————————

Day 9 Invocation

Dear Creator, the angels and allies of wealth, Yeyayel, and Lauviah, I ask you to bring me the success, fortune, fame, and celebrity in alignment with my highest and best potential.

Bring me the right people who respect and celebrate me and my work so that I can be of greater service. Release me from any obstacles blocking me from feeling more respected and celebrated. I thank you for coming to me.

❧

Next, either you can listen to the free guided meditation audio that I have provided to you for day 9 or you can perform the following meditation on your own.

Audio meditation available at
AngelWealthMagic.com/Resources

——————— ❧ ———————

Day 9 Meditation

Close your eyes, center yourself, sit quietly, and say both Yeyayel's and Lauviah's names three times and imagine that one of the angels stands at your right side and the other stands at your left side.

The message these angels bring to you is: "Remember who you are. You have permission to walk through life as proud as a rooster is of its brood. Walk with pride, dear one, and open your mind to your true power."

Allow a kinship with these angels to arise, as if they were dear old friends. Speak to both of them about any fears or money worries that you have. Ask them to release you from these worries and help you find peace as you walk your best path toward achieving greater wealth. Ask them to help you feel celebrated and respected in your life and your work. Allow this conversation to continue until you feel like you have been heard.

Breathe deeply and imagine these angels lifting out old gunk from your heart, mind, and body. With every exhale, release any resistance you have to shining your light, standing out in a crowd, or even being seen by others.

Allow these beautiful angels to fill you with the light of success and of celebrity. See, feel, or sense it in your body. Embody this light and allow yourself to experience what it feels like to truly be respected and celebrated by others for who you are and for the work you do.

Thank these angelic helpers for assisting you, and release them in peace, knowing that they are getting to work for you behind the scenes. Wait until you feel, sense, or know that they have gone.

Now, gently come back fully to your body and to the space around you.

✤

Remember, you have just as much right as anyone else to be loved, respected, and celebrated for all that you are. Let these angels help.

Now grab your grimoire, write "Day 9" on it, write the amount of cash you are manifesting, and circle it. Then sit quietly and write any thoughts and feelings that came up for you.

Now that you are done with day 9, keep your eyes and ears open for signs that your wealth magic is working.

May you receive all the wealth you are asking for and more.

See you tomorrow on day 10.

Day 10

Hodahdiah and Sekeshiah

Big Manifesting and Big Money

Welcome to day 10!
You've been working hard over the past nine days to open up your inner life to attracting wealth and a wealthy attitude. And you are really learning how to enlist the help of all manner of amazing angels and allies to make your dreams a reality.

Since today we are nearing the end of this adventure, we are going to offer you a major rocket-fuel boost to your wealth intentions by giving you the ability to more purely manifest your stated desires. Today we are going to combine the awesome manifesting power of Hodahdiah with the powers of Sekeshiah, who is an angel of abundance.

Hodahdiah represents the experience of a variety of angel powers all wrapped up in one. This angel will make your intentions more likely to manifest by shifting the energy inside you. This shift will help fertilize your inner-reality garden so that your wealth intentions can really thrive. This angel doesn't just give you manifesting power; they offer you *ultra-mega*-miraculous manifesting power.

Like Hodahdiah, Sekeshiah combines the powers of many angels, and they magnify and multiply the fertility of your wealth garden. This angel brings you the knowing that all is well, and that you will effortlessly receive everything you need to get you to the next level. They can help you be a cash magnet and do away with your money fears. They can help you open up to the infinite flow of abundance that's all around you all the time and help you say yes to receiving more of it. Blessings flow to you when you work with this angel, and you will be able to receive these blessings effortlessly.

Ready to work with these mega angels? Good, then let's call them in.

Say the invocation below out loud.

———————— ⚜ ————————

Day 10 Invocation

Dear Creator, angels and allies of wealth, and Hodahdiah and Sekeshiah, I ask for your help in making my life a more fertile playground for manifesting abundance. Help me release any beliefs interrupting this flow and help my life brim with abundance at all levels. Show me the miracle of manifesting true abundance with ease. I thank you for hearing my plea.

⚜

Next, either you can listen to the free guided meditation audio that I have provided to you for day 10 or you can perform the following meditation on your own.

Audio meditation available at
AngelWealthMagic.com/Resources

<hr>

Day 10 Meditation

Identify the parts of your body that feel burdened and tired. Take a few moments and let your body show you how hard you have worked in life. You have fought for your health, for love and respect, for your family and good friends, and even for the cash you already have. Relax, and allow your body to show you where all this hard work and tiredness lives inside you.

Say Hodahdiah's and Sekeshiah's names three times and get a sense that they have entered the room with you.

Take a moment to share how tired you are of anything you have struggled with. Pour your heart out and be honest with them.

Ask them to take this struggle away. Beg them, even. And ask them to replace all this struggle with the flow and ease you desire.

Now I have a message to share from Hodahdiah and Sekeshiah. Allow yourself to feel the truth of this message: "Manifesting your next level of wealth doesn't have to feel like hard work. It can be joyful and flow with ease and perfect timing." This is the gift they bring to you today. Do you accept it?

Now it's time to make a powerful choice: the choice to radically and miraculously manifest abundance. Say out loud: "I choose to be wealthy." Feel the choice you made, and mean it. Let yourself open up to the energy of flow and ease within you, and feel how simple it is to cocreate this wealth with the Divine.

Allow these two extraordinary angels to give you an infusion of even more energy of abundance. Envision them filling all areas of your life with the flow and ease that come with manifesting true wealth. Witness, sense, and feel yourself, your life, and your bank account expanding in abundance with the help of these wealth allies.

When you feel like this process is done and you're getting the vibes of more wealth and abundance, thank these angels and sense your renewed commitment to allowing all the best things to happen to you with flow and ease. You can let these angels go in peace, and then come back to the room and your body.

✤

Now grab your grimoire, write "Day 10" on it, write the amount of cash you are manifesting, and circle it. Then sit quietly and write any thoughts and feelings that came up for you.

Shazam! Now that you are done with day 10, keep your eyes and ears open for signs that your wealth magic is working.

May you receive all the wealth you are asking for and more.

See you tomorrow for our last day of this wealth ritual, day 11!

Day 11

Omael, Jupiter, and Cahetel

Magnify and Multiply Your Harvest

Welcome to our last day of this wealth ritual!

Over the past ten days, we have covered a lot of bases to help you find the right head and heart space to cultivate your inner wealth garden. The angels have helped you clear the weeds and fertilize your intentions so that the wealth seeds you are planting for this ritual can actually grow.

Today we work with not one, not two, but *three* allies to help you both materialize and supercharge your magical wealth intention. I can't wait for you to meet this trifecta of awesome wealth allies...because they are powerful individually but are a serious triple treat when you work with them together.

Are you ready?

Let's first meet Omael. This angel alone represents so many of the intentions and qualities that we have already worked toward on our journey together. Omael helps you stay beautifully optimistic in the face of adversity and through perceived failure. They also give you willpower to finish what you start and to avoid distractions, even when things are tumultuous. They help you heal from the bad experiences of the past that may be interfering with your ability to move audaciously forward in your life. In addition to all this, this angel has been traditionally known to help you *materialize* your intentions, taking them from simple thought forms all the way to physical reality. Now, what's cool about this angel is that they don't just help you materialize your intentions; they will help you *magnify* them. Nothing wrong with multiplying your harvest, right? Especially when it comes to building longer-term, sustainable, and even generational wealth.

Now let's meet our surprise guest: Jupiter. No, Jupiter isn't an angel, and I was actually shocked that Jupiter came forward during this ritual, but as I sat with it, I could see the absolute genius that Spirit has in store for you on this last day of wealth awesomeness. Jupiter is the largest planet in our solar system, and in astrology, it represents the energies of growth, expansion, prosperity, good fortune, luck, and, yes, even miracles. Such perfect qualities to support your amazing wealth intentions!

As if those two allies aren't enough, I want you to meet Cahetel. Cahetel helps make manifest not just your will and intentions but also God's or Creator's will for you. Sometimes what we *think* we want is different from what we truly want at a deeper level, and this angel can help your intentions be in complete alignment with the Divine Will. They can also set you free from the inner demons that block success. And last but definitely not least, they can ensure that you receive the biggest harvest possible from all the hard work you put in.

These three bring such an incredible weaving of magical wealth powers to this last day of your wealth magic ritual! Remember to summon your own juiciest power and knock today's ritual out of the park. Conjure that emotion about your intention, remember your *whys*, and really put your back into this one to bring some energy to it.

Ready?

Say the invocation below out loud and welcome in the awesomeness.

Day 11 Invocation

Dear Creator, angels and allies of wealth, Omael, Jupiter, and Cahetel, I ask you to manifest my wealth intention. Please bring it to me swiftly and easily. Help me receive the biggest and best harvest possible. I am ready to receive all the goodness that the Divine has to offer me. I ask that all this be done under the direction of the Most High and in accordance with the Divine Will. I thank you for your assistance.

Next, either you can listen to the free guided meditation audio that I have provided to you for day 11 or you can perform the following meditation on your own.

Audio meditation available at
AngelWealthMagic.com/Resources

———————————— ❧ ————————————

Day 11 Meditation

For our final day, I want you to face your palms toward each other and imagine a ball of light about the size of a basketball beginning to form between your hands. Next, I want you to project your intention for this ritual into the center of this ball. Put all your passion, desire, and emotion surrounding your intention into it, as if you are inflating this ball with your intention. You may be able to feel this energy forming between your hands. Take your time, and if you like, you can even speak your intention and prayers into this basketball-size light bubble. Wait until you feel like it's full of all that wealth goodness.

Next, close your eyes and call on Omael, Jupiter, and Cahetel to appear in front of you. If you want to make the experience stronger, say each of their names three times: "Omael, Omael, Omael; Jupiter, Jupiter, Jupiter; Cahetel, Cahetel, Cahetel." Thank them for coming and ask them to magnify and multiply these intentions through the great power of…you guessed it…love.

Once you feel that Omael, Jupiter, and Cahetel have heard your request, I want you to take a big breath and throw that basketball full of your wealth intentions over to these heavies. Witness, feel, sense, and know that they received it and are gladly taking it from you so that they can get to work for you.

Thank them and release the trio and your intentions to the universe. Let yourself feel the truth of this.

Now that you have put all this great work into your wealth ritual, know that it is in the Creator's hands. Let your mind and body feel the comfort of being supported by all these invisible allies.

Remember that over the past eleven days, you have summoned the best of the best to work their wealth magic for you. So now, there's only one thing left for you to do, and this step just may be more important than all the rest. It's time for you to party! You did it! Your angels and allies are celebrating with you too!

To close down this ritual, take out your grimoire and write in "Day 11." Jot down everything that you felt, sensed, or experienced on this day, and then write your angels and allies a love letter in your grimoire. Thank them for any new insights, inspirations, healing, and manifestations you have already had, and keep thanking them throughout the day. Know that your intentions over the past eleven days weren't just heard — they will also be delivered and multiplied.

Today you may want to create your own closing ritual and serve up a special offering of gratitude to all the allies of wealth you have met through this process. Celebrate with the angels and celebrate all the gifts that are on their way to you.

Great work over these past eleven days! I hope you enjoyed the ride. And this ritual is just the beginning. Keep choosing a healthy, wealthy mindset and healthy, wealthy habits, and watch your harvest multiply for years to come.

Miraculous wealth juju comin' at ya!

Conclusion

Wealth Magic After-Party

*How to Keep Expanding Your Wealth Magic
in Every Area of Your Life*

Now that you've officially hired the angels and allies of wealth to help you manifest more cash money, how does it feel? You may have already had some pretty amazing results, or perhaps you are still waiting. Either way, by working the processes in this book, you have set in motion powerful forces to help you attract new possibilities for wealth.

At this stage in the work, it's a good idea for you to reflect on any results you've had thus far. Do you feel more peace about yourself on the inside and about your life? Do you worry less about money or your future? Do you have more gratitude for your life? Or feel more supported by life? Did some cool things happen for you? Sometimes the best outcomes in the initial stages of successful wealth magic are psychological and emotional shifts. These kinds of successes can sometimes be easy to miss, so slow down and notice even the smallest shifts. You may not be aware of any obvious developments, or perhaps you have already had a miraculous manifestation of cash. Whatever the case, this reflection time allows your magic to grow and will help you fine-tune your awareness.

Now, check in to see if any of these questions ring true:

- Do you feel more hopeful about your future?
- Do you have less anxiety about money?
- Do you have a little more confidence in yourself?
- Do you feel more committed to acquiring more wealth?
- Do you love cash a little more?
- Are your thoughts a little or a lot more positive about your life and your potential?
- Do you feel even a tad worthier of having more in life?

My hope is that you have at least noticed a small positive shift. But even if you said no to every single one of these questions, it's OK. You can repeat this ritual process as often you'd like.

I also want to send you away with additional support before we end our time together. Aligning your life with sustainable wealth takes patience and is a constant work in progress. Your beautiful wealth magic work found in this book is just the beginning. Here are some tips on how to keep your wealth garden growing indefinitely:

- **Follow the joy.** You were likely born from an orgasm, so why not lead an orgasmic life? Your path to finding deep purpose is closely aligned with the parts of life that light you up and bring you joy. I invite you to consider creating your next level of wealth with this in mind. How fun would it be to earn a healthy living by doing work that's absolutely awesome? Spoiler alert: it's pretty dang fun. So let your heart and mind dance with the possibility of doing work and creating offerings for others that you absolutely love so that it won't feel like "work" at all.

- **Keep building a relationship with the angels.** Commit to building a relationship with angels, with Spirit, and with other amazing invisible allies. They are there for you and can help you not just with wealth but with anything at all. Talk to them all day. Remember that they are with you right now. Keep speaking with them. You are never alone, and the more you communicate with them, the more you will experience this as truth.

- **Go all in.** Don't be half-assed about your wealth making. Commit to wealth with your *whole* ass. Remember, angels can't do the heavy lifting for you. Sometimes you will be guided to make small, incremental shifts, and sometimes your guidance will demand bold, courageous — even audacious — actions to align your life with your highest potential. Allow yourself to say yes to these urges and move flexibly on this journey toward wealth.

- **Commit to developing a wealth mindset.** I gave you plenty of ideas for this in chapter 5; however, it's worth mentioning again. Sustainable wealth begins on the inside. Note the areas where you still need improvement, and keep asking the angels to help you create a mindset that's conducive to extraordinary wealth.

- **Block the inner demons.** Beat them at their own game. Pay attention to the dialogue in your head, and when you catch yourself trying to harsh on your own vibe with negative thoughts, know that it's really the tricksters at play. Don't let the inner demons stop you.

- **Listen to the sweet, soft voice inside you.** Your own intuition is one of your greatest allies. Develop your intuition, and learn to *trust* it. Take classes or workshops or go on retreats to help you nurture this connection. This tip alone could set your next-level life on fire.

- **Find community that inspires you.** As I mentioned a bit earlier in the book, building a network of wealthy and success-minded folks is powerful. Surround yourself with amazing and supportive people. If you can't find folks locally, there's a whole wide world out there. Seek amazing online communities if need be. You can find some on my website at CorinGrillo.com.

- **Stay in gratitude, and count your blessings frequently.** A grateful heart stays receptive to abundance. Open your eyes to the good medicine and the blessings that surround you in every moment, and you will begin to align yourself with the abundant flow of nature itself.

In closing, I feel compelled to share that I know life can sometimes get lonely, and it's easy to feel lost, confused, and forgotten. As a matter of fact, you may be so broke right now that it hurts, but I want you to know that it can get better — way better. You have definitely not been forgotten, even if it sometimes feels like you have been. I'm hoping that this book has given you a new sense of hope for what's possible for you in this life. Keep opening up your heart, mind, and life to all the good things and to the angels. And please remember that *you are not alone.*

It's my deepest hope that this is just the beginning of a beautiful adventure you share with the angels. May you receive everything you are asking for and more, and may the work you have begun here bring you ever closer to your heart and closer to your purpose. The universe is conspiring to bring you wealth and all the good things life has to offer. Open your arms and *let it in.*

On angels' wings we soar together, never alone again.

Corin

Acknowledgments

This book has come together with inspiration from the medicine that is animated through my human teachers and my invisible allies.

To my husband (the Bear) and children: Nothing has meant more to me than the open-ended support each of you has given to me to be authentic and real. Thank you for always allowing me to wave my full freak-flag nature and for calling me out when things go out of balance. Thank you for inspiring me to be the best mom and happiest version of myself along the way.

To Corey Eaton: Thank you playing with me, for challenging me, for loving me, and for bringing me your good Wolf medicine and strength, and especially for biting my neck when I'm at risk of taking life too seriously. This is the best medicine.

To Maia Driver, my first editor: Thank you for coping with all my spiral writing like a boss and decoding what I was trying to say to give these chapters a solid framework. You are a complete badass.

To the team at New World Library: My, how I love you. I feel your trust in me. I honor you for believing in this brown woman from the hood and for seeing my value at a time on the planet when so many brown voices are suppressed in spiritual spaces. You all have treated me so kindly, respectfully, and generously, and I am forever grateful for this opportunity.

To my father, Pascual S. Cartagena, and to Lupe, my bonus mother: Our families coming together has meant the world to me. We are stronger in numbers. Dad, thank you for toughening me up to get me ready for the world. Thank you for always letting me be me, and thank you for bringing me the awareness of money growing up. I've always felt you cheering me on.

To my siblings, Noni and Corrinne: I see myself through both of you. I'm so grateful for your excessive love and support. You give me the strength to be me, because I know that all I have to do is say "the word" and a pack of Puerto Rican / Mexican wolves will be surrounding me with your fierceness.

To my ancestors and angels: I feel your power animate through me. Thank you for serving and protecting me and my family. Thank you for all the miracles. Please share this gift with others.

California Condor Spirit: Thank you for your newest, deepest teachings at Casa Condor, our retreat center near Mount Shasta. And for showing me that revealing inner wealth is one of my greatest offerings to others. Thank you for showing me more of who I am, more of my power, and more of how I can serve others at even deeper levels.

About the Author

Corin Grillo, MA, LMFT, is a Chicana and Puerto Rican mother, licensed psychotherapist, speaker, and transformational leader. A miracle saved her life, cured her of lifelong depression, and awakened her spiritual gifts. Since that day, Corin has been committed to teaching tens of thousands around the world about the profound magic that lives inside them and how to set it free.

Corin leads transformational retreats at Casa Condor in Mount Shasta, California, and other sacred sites internationally. She is also the founder of the Angel Alchemy Academy, which is dedicated to helping other seekers deepen their intuition and natural healing abilities and unlock their deeper mission.

She transforms lives with inspired, down-to-earth spiritual wisdom and helps people reach their full potential in leadership and life by creating an authentic, non-religious relationship with the Divine and with nature, as well as a connection with their own angels and ancestral roots.

You can learn more about Corin's work and join her angel community at CorinGrillo.com.